Edexcel Anthology of Poetry

Relationships

As everyone knows, analysing relationships is brilliant fun.
But analysing poems about relationships? That can be daunting.

Not to worry. This brilliant book guides you through the entire cluster — form,
structure, language, themes, context... the lot. And because it's from CGP,
we get straight to the point, with no needless rambling.

We've also included plenty of practice questions to test you on what you've learned,
plus a whole section of advice to help you score a top grade in the exam.
It's the perfect partner to your poetry studies, so don't leave it on the shelf...

The Poetry Guide

CONTENTS

How to Use this Book 1

Section One — The Poems

La Belle Dame Sans Merci — John Keats.............................. 2
A Child to his Sick Grandfather — Joanna Baillie 4
She Walks in Beauty — Lord Byron..................................... 6
A Complaint — William Wordsworth.................................... 8
Neutral Tones — Thomas Hardy 10
Sonnet 43 — Elizabeth Barrett Browning 12
My Last Duchess — Robert Browning 14
First Date – She / First Date – He — Wendy Cope 16
Valentine — Carol Ann Duffy 18
One Flesh — Elizabeth Jennings 20
i wanna be yours — John Cooper Clarke............................... 22
Love's Dog — Jen Hadfield 24
Nettles — Vernon Scannell 26
The Manhunt — Simon Armitage 28
My Father Would Not Show Us — Ingrid de Kok 30
Practice Questions 32

Section Two — Themes

Romantic Love.. 36
Family Relationships 38
Memory 39
Desire and Longing.. 40
Adoration... 41
Death and Suffering... 42
Distance and Separation 44
Negative Emotions 45
Practice Questions 46

Section Three — Poetic Techniques

Forms of Poetry 49
Poetic Devices 50
Imagery... 52
Use of Sound 54
Rhyme and Rhythm... 55
Voice 56
Beginnings of Poems.. 57
Endings of Poems 58
Practice Questions 59

CONTENTS

Section Four — Exam Advice

The Poetry Exam 62
How to Structure Your Answer 63
How to Answer the Question 64
Planning Your Answer 67
Sample Answer 68

Section Five — Improving and Marking Sample Answers

Adding Quotes and Developing Points.................................. 70
Mark Scheme.. 72
Marking Answer Extracts 73
Marking a Whole Answer... 75

Glossary... 77
Index 79
Answers 80

Published by CGP

Editors:
Izzy Bowen
Tom Carney
Emma Crighton
Gabrielle Richardson
Matt Topping

With thanks to Stephanie Halifax and Sean Walsh for the proofreading.
With thanks to Ana Pungartnik for the copyright research.

Acknowledgements:

Cover quote from 'Sonnet 43' by Elizabeth Barrett Browning.

'First Date - She and First Date - He' by Wendy Cope from _'Family Values'_ published by Faber & Faber, 2012.

'Valentine' from _Mean Time_ by Carol Ann Duffy. Published by Picador, 2013. Copyright © Carol Ann Duffy. Reproduced by permission of the author c/o Rogers, Coleridge & White Ltd., 20 Powis Mews, London W11 1JN.

'One Flesh' by Elizabeth Jennings from _New Collected Poems_, Carcanet, 2002.
Reproduced by permission of David Higham Associates.

'i wanna be yours' Words and Music by John Cooper Clarke, Martin Hannett, Stephen Hopkins © 1982. Reproduced by permission of EMI Music Publishing Ltd, London W1F 9LD

'Love's Dog' by Jen Hadfield from _Nigh-No-Place, Bloodaxe Books, 2008._
Reproduced by permission of Bloodaxe Books. www.bloodaxebooks.com

'Nettles' by Vernon Scannell from _Collected Poems 1950-1993_ (Faber).

'The Manhunt (Laura's Poem)' by Simon Armitage from _The Not Dead_, 2008 published by Pomona.
Reprinted by permission of Pomona.

'My Father Would Not Show Us' from _Seasonal Fires: new and selected poems_, Ingrid de Kok, Umuzi Cape Town and Seven Stories Press, New York, 2006. Reproduced by permission of Ingrid de Kok.

Every effort has been made to locate copyright holders and obtain permission to reproduce sources. For those sources where it has been difficult to trace the copyright holder of the work, we would be grateful for information. If any copyright holder would like us to make an amendment to the acknowledgements, please notify us and we will gladly update the book at the next reprint. Thank you.

ISBN: 978 1 78908 001 8
Printed by Elanders Ltd, Newcastle upon Tyne.
Clipart from Corel®

Based on the classic CGP style created by Richard Parsons.

How to Use this Book

This book is for anyone studying the 'Relationships' cluster of the Edexcel GCSE English Literature Poetry Anthology. This book tells you what you need to know to answer the Poetry Anthology question in the exam.

You need to know the poems really well

You need to know all fifteen poems <u>in depth</u>. Read each one carefully <u>over and over again</u>, and jot down your <u>own ideas</u> about it. This book will help you <u>understand</u> the poems and develop your ideas:

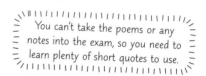
You can't take the poems or any notes into the exam, so you need to learn plenty of short quotes to use.

- <u>Section One</u> guides you through each poem in the cluster — read the <u>notes</u> on what each poem <u>means</u>, its main <u>features</u>, and the <u>attitudes</u> and <u>feelings</u> it conveys.
- Answer the <u>questions</u> about each poem — these will help you develop a <u>personal response</u> to it.
- When you feel that you know the poems <u>well</u>, have a go at the <u>questions</u> at the end of the section. They'll help you identify any <u>gaps</u> in your knowledge of the poems.

In the exam, you have to compare poems

1) The Poetry Anthology question will give you <u>one</u> poem from the 'Relationships' cluster, and ask you to <u>choose another</u> to compare it to, usually based on a certain theme.

2) In <u>Section Two</u> the poems are grouped by <u>theme</u>, to give you some ideas of which poems you could <u>compare</u> in the exam and what you might say about them.

3) Have a go at the <u>practice questions</u> at the end of the section to check you're up to speed with the themes of each poem.

Have a look inside the front cover for a handy summary of which themes relate to which poems.

Get to grips with the main features of each poem

1) <u>Section Three</u> is all about <u>form</u>, <u>structure</u> and <u>language</u>.

2) It looks at how different poets use techniques like <u>rhyme</u>, <u>rhythm</u> and <u>imagery</u> to create <u>effects</u> — the examiners are <u>really keen</u> for you to write about this.

3) There are some more <u>practice questions</u> at the end of the section to help you test your knowledge.

First day on the job, and Tim had already got to grips with the 'self-destruct' feature of his car.

Learn how to write a cracking exam answer

1) You need to know <u>how</u> to write a great essay <u>comparing</u> two poems:

- <u>Section Four</u> gives you loads of <u>advice</u> on how to <u>plan</u> and <u>write</u> a fantastic exam answer.
- There are several extracts from <u>sample answers</u> to show you the right way to approach the question.

2) Once you know the <u>theory</u>, put it into <u>practice</u>:

- <u>Section Five</u> lets you test your skills by <u>adding quotes</u> or <u>extending points</u> to improve essay extracts. This will help you understand how to really <u>use the poems</u> to write a <u>top-notch</u> answer.
- It also gives you some sample answers to <u>grade</u>, which will help you to improve your <u>own answers</u>.

3) There's no substitute for getting some practice at <u>writing essays</u>:

- Use what you've learnt to answer the <u>exam-style questions</u> at the end of Sections One, Two and Three.
- You don't have to write a <u>full essay</u> for every question — making a <u>detailed plan</u> is still good practice.

How to Use this Book

La Belle Dame Sans Merci

Title translates to 'the beautiful lady without mercy' and comes from a medieval romance by the French poet Alain Chartier. Knights, fair ladies, fairies and dreams are all typical features of a medieval romance.

In the first three stanzas, an anonymous speaker talks to the knight and asks questions, which are then answered by the knight in the rest of the poem.

Poem switches to the knight's voice — he narrates his own story.

"wild" contrasts with the otherwise beautiful picture of the lady. It's the first sign of danger for the knight, emphasised by its position at the end of the stanza.

Repetition of "And" throughout the poem gives the sense that the knight is telling a story out loud.

The poem uses double entendres (words or phrases with two interpretations, one of which is usually sexual). This highlights the passion and sexual attraction between the pair.

The lady is active in her temptation — she leads and the knight follows.

The knight recalls the events dreamily — repetition of "And there" puts emphasis on the place where his abandonment happened.

Caesura breaks the rhythm of the poem, mirroring how the knight's illusions are shattered.

"Pale" is repeated here to emphasise the bleakness of the situation and lifelessness of the other captives.

The lady holds great power over him — he is captive to her charm and his memory of her.

This imagery of ghostly, malnourished figures makes this seem like a nightmare.

Most of the first stanza is repeated at the end of the poem. This brings the reader back to knight's bleak reality, and they now know what's happened to him.

O what can ail thee, knight-at-arms,
    Alone and palely loitering?
The sedge has withered from the lake,
    And no birds sing.

5 O what can ail thee, knight-at-arms,
    So haggard and so woe-begone?
The squirrel's granary is full,
    And the harvest's done.

I see a lily on thy brow,
10   With anguish moist and fever-dew,
And on thy cheek a fading rose
    Fast withereth too.

I met a lady in the meads,
    Full beautiful – a faery's child,
15 Her hair was long, her foot was light,
    And her eyes were wild.

I made a garland for her head,
    And bracelets too, and fragrant zone;
She looked at me as she did love,
20   And made sweet moan.

I set her on my pacing steed,
    And nothing else saw all day long,
For sidelong would she bend, and sing
    A faery's song.

25 She found me roots of relish sweet,
    And honey wild, and manna-dew,
And sure in language strange she said –
    'I love thee true'.

She took me to her elfin grot,
30   And there she wept and sighed full sore,
And there I shut her wild wild eyes
    With kisses four.

And there she lulled me asleep
    And there I dreamed – Ah! woe betide! –
35 The latest dream I ever dreamt
    On the cold hill side.

I saw pale kings, and princes too,
    Pale warriors, death-pale were they all;
They cried – 'La Belle Dame sans Merci
40   Thee hath in thrall!'

I saw their starved lips in the gloam,
    With horrid warning gapèd wide,
And I awoke and found me here,
    On the cold hill's side.

45 And this is why I sojourn here
    Alone and palely loitering,
Though the sedge is withered from the lake,
    And no birds sing.

The knight is introduced as lost and abandoned, hinting that something has gone wrong. Knights are traditionally noble and brave, so his despair is unexpected and unusual.

Descriptions of lonely, desolate surroundings show the knight is surrounded by winter and set a bleak, lifeless tone for the poem.

Flower metaphors reflect the knight's situation. Lilies are very pale and are often associated with death — the knight is pale and suffering. Roses are vibrant and symbolise beauty and love, but here the rose withers, suggesting loss of love.

Beautiful and idealistic descriptions are typical of the Romantic era (see p.8). They often hinted at the presence of another world.

This image of beautiful flowers contrasts with the "fading rose" in line 11. She is alluring and lively compared to the dispirited knight.

The food the lady gives the knight and the language she uses are both unfamiliar — she seems mysterious and otherworldly.

It's unclear why she weeps — she might be overcome with passion, or it could hint that she knows she cannot escape the cycle and is doomed to entrap men forever.

Repetition of "wild" suggests that the speaker is entranced by the lady and her eyes — he possibly sees the danger but is powerless to resist.

The lady's previous victims appear to the knight in a dream — they show the hopelessness of his situation.

POEM DICTIONARY
sedge — grass-like plant
haggard — looking exhausted or ill
woe-begone — sad
meads — meadows
fragrant zone — a belt of flowers
manna — food given to the Israelites by God in the Bible (Exodus 16)
elfin grot — an elf's grotto or cave
in thrall — under someone's power
gloam — twilight
sojourn — stay temporarily

John Keats

John Keats was a key Romantic poet (see p.8). He wrote 'La Belle Dame Sans Merci' in 1819, not long before dying from tuberculosis (an infectious disease), which perhaps influenced the poem's bleak tone.

You've got to know what the poem's about

1) The poem describes the story of a knight who had a romantic encounter with a mysterious woman.

2) She seduced him and took him back to her magical cave, then lulled him to sleep and abandoned him.

3) In a dream, the knight saw kings, princes and warriors who had previously been seduced by the lady. They warned him of his fate, but it was too late. He awoke alone, tormented by the memory of her.

4) Keats reverses the traditional medieval romance — normally a knight falls in love with a beautiful lady and has to win her over, but here the knight is seduced by the beautiful woman and she ruins him.

Learn about the form, structure and language

1) **FORM** — The poem is a ballad — these traditionally tell entertaining stories. The ABCB rhyme scheme and iambic tetrameter are typical of ballads — they are simple and regular to aid the storytelling. Keats uses shorter last lines in each stanza. This disrupts the iambic tetrameter, mirroring the knight's disturbance and reflecting how the romance is not a traditional one.

2) **STRUCTURE** — The poem is structured as a question and answer narrative. An anonymous speaker appears in the first three stanzas to question the knight, and the rest of the poem is the knight's response. The repetition of the first stanza creates a cyclical structure — the knight is back in the bleak surroundings from the start of the poem, which hints that he is doomed to stay there forever.

3) **CONTRAST** — There is a stark contrast between the knight's present and past situations, e.g. the "cold hill side" of the knight's current surroundings and the idyllic, abundant "meads" he describes from when he was with the lady. This emphasises how his situation has drastically changed.

4) **SUPERNATURAL IMAGERY** — What happens to the knight is never fully explained, but there is an impression that it was perhaps something magical. The lady is described so dreamily by the knight that she seems almost mythical. Supernatural imagery adds to the aura of mystery that surrounds her.

Remember the feelings and attitudes in the poem

1) **DESPAIR** — The knight feels a keen sense of loss after his experience with the mysterious lady — he is "loitering" aimlessly, unsure what to do. He seems lost, abandoned and helpless.

2) **INFATUATION** — The knight's infatuation (passionate obsession) with the lady is clear. His descriptions of her physical appearance suggest perfection, but the warning of her "wild" eyes, and his failure to act upon it, indicate the dangerous side of this infatuation.

Go a step further and give a personal response

Have a go at answering these questions to help you come up with your own ideas about the poem:

Q1.   Consider the fate of the lady in the poem. What hints are there that she is also doomed?

Q2.   Why do you think Keats uses an anonymous speaker at the beginning of the poem?

Q3.   Do you think the context of the poet's illness has an effect on the poem? Explain your answer.

Desire and longing, suffering, separation...

You can compare the knight's desire for the lady in the poem with that of the speaker in 'She Walks in Beauty'. Suffering caused by love is also shown by the speaker's bleak surroundings in 'Neutral Tones'.

A Child to his Sick Grandfather

The narrator addresses their grandfather right from the start — immediate focus on him and his illness.

Painful to see him so unwell — also frustrating for the child who remembers how their grandfather used to be.

"But now" is short and sudden, snapping the focus back to the present. It clearly separates the past from the present and helps to highlight the differences between the two.

The exclamations indicate the child's shock and distress at the physical signs of their grandfather's frailty.

Conjures images of witches — shows childish perspective and imagination.

Repetition emphasises how many people are affected by the grandfather's illness.

Sibilance and the repeated soft 'f' sound in "doff" and "softly" make this sound like a whisper, echoing the child's promise to be quiet.

Child affectionately promises to look after him if he gets better — trying to bargain with him.

This story likely involves the threat of death. This could show the child's lack of understanding — they choose to tell their dying grandfather a story about death.

The question mark implies that the narrator is struggling to get his attention — perhaps they can see that he is losing consciousness.

Monosyllabic, simple language is emphatic and shows the gravity of the moment. It hints that the child can't fully describe what is happening.

The final couplet is only a half-rhyme — the full rhyme would be 'dead.' This reinforces the implication that the grandfather has died.

Grand-dad, they say you're old and frail,
Your stocked legs begin to fail:
Your knobbed stick (that was my horse)
Can scarce support your bended corse,
5   While back to wall, you lean so sad,
        I'm vexed to see you, dad.

You used to smile and stroke my head,
And tell me how good children did;
But now, I wot not how it be,
10   You take me seldom on your knee,
Yet ne'ertheless I am right glad,
        To sit beside you, dad.

How lank and thin your beard hangs down!
Scant are the white hairs on your crown;
15   How wan and hollow are your cheeks!
Your brow is rough with crossing breaks;
But yet, for all his strength be fled,
        I love my own old dad.

The housewives round their potions brew,
20   And gossips come to ask for you;
And for your weal each neighbour cares,
And good men kneel, and say their prayers;
And everybody looks so sad,
        When you are ailing, dad.

25   You will not die and leave us then?
Rouse up and be our dad again.
When you are quiet and laid in bed,
We'll doff our shoes and softly tread;
And when you wake we'll aye be near
30   To fill old dad his cheer.

When through the house you shift your stand,
I'll lead you kindly by the hand;
When dinner's set I'll with you bide,
And aye be serving at your side;
35   And when the weary fire turns blue,
        I'll sit and talk with you.

I have a tale both long and good,
About a partlet and her brood,
And cunning greedy fox that stole
40   By dead of midnight through a hole,
Which slyly to the hen-roost led –
        You love a story, dad?

And then I have a wondrous tale
Of men all clad in coats of mail,
45   With glittering swords – you nod, I think?
Your fixed eyes begin to wink;
Down on your bosom sinks your head –
        You do not hear me, dad.

The first stanza is focused on the present, but the parentheses show the narrator's mind switching to fond memories of the past.

The grandfather is described as if he's already dead, emphasising just how frail he is.

"dad" is an affectionate abbreviation of "Grand-dad" — it shows how familiar the narrator is with their grandfather.

Classic image of a child sitting on their grandfather's knee — their physical relationship has had to change but the child loves their grandfather just the same.

Monosyllabic language — despite the physical changes, nothing has changed emotionally. The speaker still has a simple, childlike love for their grandfather.

Simple, innocent description — reminder that a child is speaking.

Change in tone as the child appeals directly to the grandfather. Stanza begins with hopeful question, followed by an imperative, as if they are trying to persuade him to get better.

The personified "weary fire" perhaps mirrors the ageing grandfather. The image of the fire turning "blue" could foreshadow him passing away.

Role reversal — the child is now the one telling stories to their grandfather.

The narrator perhaps attempts to copy the way their grandfather used to tell them stories — both to appeal to him and to avoid the reality of the situation.

POEM DICTIONARY
stocked — wearing stockings (close-fitting trousers)
knobbed — lumpy
corse — corpse
vexed — frustrated or worried
wot — know
lank — limp, lifeless
wan — pale or tired-looking
weal — well-being
doff — remove an item of clothing
bide — remain or stay
partlet — hen
clad in — wearing
mail — armour made of metal rings

Section One — The Poems

Joanna Baillie

Joanna Baillie (1762-1851) was a Scottish poet and playwright. She was well-respected in her lifetime, and her work has gained even more recognition since. 'A Child to his Sick Grandfather' was published in 1790.

You've got to know what the poem's about

1) The narrator is addressing their elderly grandfather on his sick bed.

2) The narrator describes their grandfather's frailty and how things are different from how they used to be. They are desperate for their grandfather to recover, and try different ways of rousing him.

3) The end of the poem is ambiguous, but it's implied that the grandfather dies in the final stanza.

Learn about the form, structure and language

1) **FORM** — The poem's regular AABBCC rhyme scheme and consistent stanza length mirror the reliablity of the grandparent. However, the poem also uses half-rhymes (e.g. lines 17-18), and the last lines of each stanza are shorter — this could reflect how the grandfather is becoming weaker and fading away.

2) **STRUCTURE** — The first stanza introduces the grandfather and his illness, then the poem moves from memories of the past to the present. It is a fairly simple structure, which guides the reader through the story and ends by hinting at the grandfather's death.

3) **CHILDLIKE VOICE** — The language in the poem is often monosyllabic ("I love my own old dad"), which could suggest a young narrator. However, some stanzas include more complex language ("rough with crossing breaks"). Although the reader is never told the age of the narrator, this contrast could indicate that the child is older but perhaps not mature enough to fully process the grandfather's death.

4) **DIRECT ADDRESS** — The repetition of "dad" at the end of almost every stanza makes it sound as though the narrator is trying to keep their grandfather's attention. They plead with their grandfather, ask him questions and use imperatives in their attempt to engage and energise him.

Remember the feelings and attitudes in the poem

1) INNOCENCE — The child in the poem is struggling to understand their grandfather's illness, and the reader sees their innocence when they try to bargain with him ("You will not die and leave us then?"). The child believes that they can turn the situation around by negotiating with him.

2) SADNESS — The narrator struggles to come to terms with the illness of a loved one. They care about their grandfather so much that it is upsetting to see him so frail, and unthinkable that he might die.

Go a step further and give a personal response

Have a go at answering these questions to help you come up with your own ideas about the poem:

Q1.   What mood does the title set for the poem?

Q2.   What effect does the rhyme scheme have on the overall tone of the poem?

Q3.   Why is the use of the word "crown" (line 14) significant?

Family relationships, death, memory...

The death of a close family member is also explored in 'My Father Would Not Show Us'. 'Nettles' also focuses on caring family relationships, with the parent in the poem trying to protect their injured child.

She Walks in Beauty

The poem is narrated in the present tense, making the woman's beauty seem eternal.

The narrator uses the extended simile of the night to describe the woman's appearance. He might be talking about the colour of her skin or hair, or the clothes she's wearing.

Imagery suggests the woman's beauty is pure. Alliteration highlights the contrast between dark and light — this woman represents the best of both.

The woman is the ideal mix of dark and bright things — the poem suggests that this is better than just being one or the other.

She walks in beauty, like the night
    Of cloudless climes and starry skies;
And all that's best of dark and bright
    Meet in her aspect and her eyes:
5 Thus mellow'd to that tender light
    Which heaven to gaudy day denies.

Antithesis — the contrast between dark and light is enhanced by the line's balanced structure.

More imagery of light reinforces the idea that the woman is beautiful because she is a balance of the bright light of day and darkness.

One shade the more, one ray the less,
    Had half impair'd the nameless grace
Which waves in every raven tress,
10   Or softly lightens o'er her face;
Where thoughts serenely sweet express
    How pure, how dear their dwelling-place.

Lots of verbs to do with movement and change — "walks", "waves" and "lightens". This makes the poem sound like a lively, real-time description, rather than a rose-tinted memory.

The adjective "nameless" suggests the woman is so beautiful it can't be put into words.

The woman's beauty shows that her mind — her thoughts' "dwelling-place" — is beautiful too. It's the first bit of information that isn't about her appearance.

And on that cheek, and o'er that brow,
    So soft, so calm, yet eloquent,
15 The smiles that win, the tints that glow,
    But tell of days in goodness spent,
A mind at peace with all below,
    A heart whose love is innocent!

Use of sibilance makes these lines sound soothing, just like her "sweet" thoughts and "soft" smiles.

The narrator pays attention to different parts of the woman's face. This shows how attracted he is to her.

The words "mind" and "heart" are the first stressed syllables in these lines. The emphasis this gives them shows how much the narrator values these things.

Either innocent because she has never been in love, or because her love is virtuous and pure.

The narrator tells us that the woman has lived a moral life.

Context — Beauty and Nature
Many poets use nature to describe beauty. For example, Shakespeare does this in 'Sonnet 18', usually known by its first line "Shall I compare thee to a summer's day?" Byron uses nature differently to Shakespeare — he uses the night rather than the day to convey the woman's beauty.

Anya wasn't sure her tresses would elicit quite so much praise...

POEM DICTIONARY
climes — regions with a similar climate
aspect — appearance or face
gaudy — extravagantly, even tastelessly, bright
tress — a lock of hair
brow — forehead

Lord Byron

Byron (1788-1824) was a popular English poet, also known for his lavish lifestyle and scandalous affairs, although this poem is rather more restrained. Written in 1814, it was originally intended to be set to music.

You've got to know what the poem's about

1) The narrator describes a <u>woman</u> he's seen, taking her <u>individual body parts</u> in turn. He thinks she's incredibly <u>beautiful</u> and uses images of <u>dark</u> and <u>light</u> to emphasise how <u>perfect</u> she is.

2) He suggests that her <u>appearance</u> reflects her <u>personality</u> — she has spent her life doing <u>good things</u>.

Learn about the form, structure and language

1) **FORM** — The poem maintains a regular <u>ABABAB</u> rhyme scheme, reflecting the <u>enduring</u> nature of the woman's beauty and how she's a <u>balance</u> of different qualities. It's mostly in <u>iambic tetrameter</u> and uses a lot of <u>enjambment</u>, suggesting the narrator is <u>overwhelmed</u> by the woman's beauty.

2) **STRUCTURE** — The poem is split into <u>three stanzas</u> of equal length. As it progresses, the poem focuses less on the woman's <u>physical appearance</u> and more on her <u>inner beauty</u>. This could indicate that the narrator thinks that it is her <u>personality</u> that is most beautiful. However, his <u>evidence</u> that she is a moral person is her <u>beauty</u> — we don't know whether he knows her <u>properly</u>.

3) **CONTRASTS** — The poet employs <u>contrasts</u> to show how the woman is a <u>balance</u> of opposites, notably <u>light</u> and <u>dark</u>. He uses <u>antithesis</u> — where <u>contrasting</u> ideas are reinforced by a repeated structure — when he says that it would only take "<u>One shade</u>" more or "<u>one ray</u>" less to <u>reduce</u> her beauty.

4) **IMAGERY** — The <u>imagery</u> used in the poem, particularly that of the <u>night</u> and of <u>light and dark</u>, helps to express the narrator's view of the woman. For instance, the <u>purity</u> of the night sky reflects her <u>innocent</u> personality.

5) **LANGUAGE ABOUT THE BODY** — The narrator breaks the woman down into <u>individual body parts</u>. This shows how much he <u>admires</u> her, as he sees beauty in <u>all parts</u> of her. He seems to believe that her beauty is a <u>reflection</u> of her <u>morally good</u> character.

Remember the feelings and attitudes in the poem

1) **ADMIRATION** — The narrator is <u>amazed</u> by the woman and uses lots of different <u>images</u> and <u>techniques</u> to express her beauty. He loves how she is the <u>perfect balance</u> of different qualities and how her beauty reflects her <u>inner goodness</u>.

2) **ATTENTIVENESS** — The narrator thinks about the <u>different parts</u> of the woman's appearance and personality. He breaks down his description to look at each part of her <u>separately</u>. This emphasises the woman's <u>perfection</u>, as every part of her <u>deserves</u> his praise.

Go a step further and give a personal response

Have a go at <u>answering</u> these <u>questions</u> to help you come up with <u>your own ideas</u> about the poem:

Q1.   Why do you think the narrator uses the night instead of the day to describe the woman?

Q2.   Do you think the woman's mind or body is more important to the narrator? Why?

Q3.   How is nature important in the poem?

Desire and longing, adoration, romantic love...

KEY THEMES You could try comparing the presentation of desire and longing in this poem to the speaker's desire in 'i wanna be yours'. 'Sonnet 43' also focuses on the speaker's adoration of the person they're discussing.

A Complaint

First line contains two firm statements. The semi-colon indicates an explanation or elaboration of some kind will follow.

Love is compared to a fountain — fountains are beautiful and the water in them moves rapidly, highlighting that the love the narrator felt was also beautiful and dynamic.

Narrator addresses their friend / lover directly, making the poem seem personal.

Change to the past tense — the narrator is looking back.

The metaphor of rushing water and the repetition of "flow" highlights the force and amount of love the narrator felt.

Enjambment indicates the urgency of the flowing love. It spills over the line, unrestrained.

The love showed no consideration for its own strength or the narrator's requirement of it.

Alliteration of "Blest" and "bliss" highlights how excited the speaker is and the joy they used to feel.

Exclamation shows the strength of the emotions the narrator feels when thinking about the moments they shared. It also creates a pause as the speaker reflects on the past.

Turning point — the narrator starts to explain the change, bringing the focus back to the present.

Religious language adds a divine quality to the happiness the narrator felt — it was sacred.

The fountain metaphor is replaced by the image of a well — the love has changed from a sacred "consecrated fount" to a mundane "hidden" well. This is symbolic of how the relationship has changed.

List of three lively but gentle adjectives — they emphasise that it was an enthusiastic but pure love.

Rhetorical questions are dramatic — the narrator is emphasising the extent of their sadness.

Rhetorical question creates a sense of negativity and bitterness.

The love hasn't disappeared completely — this could show that the narrator has some hope, despite the negativity in the rest of the stanza.

The sombre language here contrasts with the lively adjectives in line 10 — the love is now lifeless and hidden.

Repetition of content from the first lines of the poem acts as a conclusion. The narrator has explained the complaint and rounds off the argument, bringing the reader back to the present situation and their sense of loss.

A door is a part of a home — suggests closeness and intimacy as well as being personal.

There is a change—and I am poor;
Your love hath been, nor long ago,
A fountain at my fond heart's door,
Whose only business was to flow;
5   And flow it did; not taking heed
Of its own bounty, or my need.

What happy moments did I count!
Blest was I then all bliss above!
Now, for that consecrated fount
10 Of murmuring, sparkling, living love,
What have I? shall I dare to tell?
A comfortless and hidden well.

A well of love—it may be deep—
I trust it is,—and never dry:
15 What matter? if the waters sleep
In silence and obscurity.
—Such change, and at the very door
Of my fond heart, hath made me poor.

Context — Romanticism
Poets like Wordsworth (1770-1850), Keats (1795-1821) and Byron (1788-1824) were part of the Romantic movement. Romanticism was a movement in the late 1700s and early 1800s that had a big influence on art and literature. Romantic poets believed in prioritising emotion over reason and often focused on the power of nature.

POEM DICTIONARY
taking heed — paying attention to
bounty — generosity or reward
blest — blessed
fount — fountain
consecrated — sacred, used for a religious purpose
obscurity — ambiguity, darkness

William Wordsworth

William Wordsworth was an influential Romantic poet, and served as Poet Laureate from 1843 to his death in 1850. He lived in, and was inspired by, the Lake District. 'A Complaint' was published in 1807.

You've got to know what the poem's about

1) The narrator is <u>complaining</u> that their <u>relationship</u> with a friend or a lover has <u>changed</u> significantly.

2) They <u>struggle to accept</u> the change in the relationship and are <u>upset</u> by the situation.

3) The poem may refer to romantic love, but <u>many critics</u> believe that the poem is about Wordsworth's old friend — the poet <u>Samuel Taylor Coleridge</u>. The pair were <u>good friends</u> until Coleridge's <u>drug addiction</u> drove them apart.

Learn about the form, structure and language

1) **FORM** — The poem has a <u>regular rhyme scheme</u> (ABABCC) and is written in <u>iambic tetrameter</u>. Each sestet (stanza of six lines) ends with a <u>rhyming couplet</u>, which could represent the <u>close connection</u> between the speaker and their friend / lover. Even though the pair have drifted apart, the <u>close rhymes</u> are <u>consistent</u>, perhaps showing that the two are still <u>closely linked</u> despite the loss.

2) **STRUCTURE** — The poem moves between the <u>past</u> and the <u>present</u> — the presence of both time frames highlights how <u>raw</u> the loss is and how the narrator is still trying to <u>understand</u> it.

3) **IMAGERY OF WATER** — The poem uses contrasting <u>extended metaphors</u> of a fountain and a well. The comparison <u>explores</u> the <u>change</u> in love — it's initially described as a lively "<u>fountain</u>" but becomes a deep, "hidden <u>well</u>". <u>Water</u> is a <u>powerful</u> force, so the use of water-related metaphors to describe the love shows how <u>powerful</u> it was and how <u>deeply</u> the <u>loss</u> of it has <u>affected</u> the narrator.

4) **RELIGIOUS LANGUAGE** — <u>Religious</u> language, such as "<u>Blest</u>" and "<u>consecrated</u>", shows how highly the narrator values the love they shared. It shows love as <u>sacred</u> and as something to be <u>respected</u>.

5) **RHETORICAL DEVICES** — The use of <u>rhetoric</u> reinforces that the poem is a <u>complaint</u>. The <u>questions</u>, <u>direct address</u> and <u>repetition</u> are <u>forceful</u> and <u>persuasive</u>, and they show the <u>strength</u> of the complaint.

Remember the feelings and attitudes in the poem

1) **LOSS** — The narrator <u>grieves</u> for the <u>love</u> they have <u>lost</u>. The change is <u>introduced</u> on the first line and the <u>differences</u> between now and then become the <u>focus</u> of each stanza. However, <u>despite</u> the narrator's <u>sadness</u> at the loss, they seem to have <u>accepted</u> that the <u>change</u> is <u>irreversible</u>.

2) **JOY** — When the speaker discusses the love as it used to be, their <u>joy</u> and <u>enthusiasm</u> is evident. <u>Exclamation marks</u> and <u>lively adjectives</u>, such as "murmuring, sparkling, living", indicate their <u>strong</u>, <u>positive emotions</u> and make it clear how <u>powerful</u> their <u>love</u> was.

Go a step further and give a personal response

Have a go at <u>answering</u> these <u>questions</u> to help you come up with <u>your own ideas</u> about the poem:

Q1. Find an example of personification in the poem. What effect does it have?

Q2. What tone does the title set for the poem?

Q3. What effect do you think the caesurae have in the poem?

Distance and separation, memory, adoration...

Compare the speaker's near-religious adoration of the person they're discussing in this poem to 'Sonnet 43'. You can also look at the presentation of emotional separation in comparison to 'The Manhunt'.

Neutral Tones

The sun is drained of warmth and colour — reflects how the love has drained from their relationship.

Lack of physical movement contributes to lifeless atmosphere.

Weather reflects their feelings — they're emotionally cold towards each other.

Imagines that God has scolded the sun. This adds to the bleak mood of the poem, and hints that the narrator sees everything in a negative way.

Alliteration emphasises how the leaves are still and unmoving.

In love poems, eyes are traditionally shown to be a positive feature, but they're shown negatively here.

Alliteration and personification emphasises this impression of suffering — the lifeless ground reflects their dying relationship.

We stood by a pond that winter day,
And the sun was white, as though chidden of God,
And a few leaves lay on the starving sod;
   – They had fallen from an ash, and were gray.

The leaves are from an ash tree, but this also links to ash from a fire — their relationship has burnt out.

Enjambment mimics the movement of the eyes. The words "rove" and "Over" look and sound similar, which could reflect the boredom the other person feels.

5   Your eyes on me were as eyes that rove
Over tedious riddles of years ago;
And some words played between us to and fro
   On which lost the more by our love.

Game imagery — love should be fun and playful, but theirs became "tedious" and they "lost".

A "smile" is usually associated with living things. Linking it to death shows the addressee's complete lack of feeling towards the narrator.

The smile on your mouth was the deadest thing
10   Alive enough to have strength to die;
And a grin of bitterness swept thereby
   Like an ominous bird a-wing …

The addressee chose to let their smile die — perhaps they chose to let the love between them die too.

Imagery of a bird flying away suggests the end of the relationship.

Ellipsis represents the time when the relationship ended, in the time that passes between stanzas 3 and 4.

"keen" means sharp or strong — these lessons have been painful.

Since then, keen lessons that love deceives,
And wrings with wrong, have shaped to me
15   Your face, and the God-curst sun, and a tree,
   And a pond edged with grayish leaves.

Pessimistic generalisation that all love is deceptive.

Alliteration emphasises the narrator's pain and anguish.

Poem begins and ends by the pond — this shows how the memory of that day still affects the narrator.

The 't' in "curst" is a harsher sound than "chidden" in the first stanza — this hints that the narrator has become more bitter over time.

Other experiences of deceitful love remind them of this incident by the pond — perhaps it was the first time they experienced it.

The leaves are "grayish" because they're rotting — this reflects how their love has decayed. The repetition of this colour from the first stanza emphasises the decay.

POEM DICTIONARY
chidden — scolded
sod — grass-covered earth
rove — wander
thereby — by
a-wing — flying
wrings — causes someone distress
curst — cursed

Bert looked like a twit when he saw Simone again after twoo years.

Thomas Hardy

Thomas Hardy (1840-1928) was born in Dorset. 'Neutral Tones' was written in 1867 and published in 1898 as part of his *Wessex Poems and Other Verses* collection. Lots of his work is regarded as pessimistic and bleak.

You've got to know what the poem's about

1) The narrator <u>remembers</u> a day when they stood by a pond with their lover. It's an <u>unpleasant</u> memory — it's clear that the relationship was <u>failing</u> and about to come to an <u>end</u>.

2) The lover seems <u>bored</u> with the narrator and has fallen <u>out of love</u> with them.

3) Whenever the narrator has been hurt by love since, they <u>remember</u> that day by the pond.

Learn about the form, structure and language

1) **FORM** — The poem is written from the point of view of someone addressing a <u>past lover</u>. The <u>first</u> and <u>last</u> lines of each stanza <u>rhyme</u>, which reflects how the <u>memory</u> of a <u>past</u> experience returns to affect the narrator in the <u>present</u>. The <u>indented final line</u> of each stanza <u>slows</u> the pace of the poem by creating a <u>pause</u> — this hints at their <u>sadness</u> that the relationship failed.

2) **STRUCTURE** — The first three stanzas centre around a specific <u>memory</u>, then there's a <u>time jump</u> to the final stanza where the narrator <u>reflects</u> on love in general. The poem <u>ends</u> where it <u>began</u>, with the image of a <u>pond</u> — this <u>cyclical structure</u> represents how the speaker has been repeatedly <u>hurt</u> by love <u>since</u> that day by the pond, and how these experiences always <u>remind</u> them of that day.

3) **LANGUAGE ABOUT SUFFERING** — Although the 'neutral' tone of the poem is <u>never broken</u>, it's clear that the narrator has <u>strong emotions</u> about that day by the pond — language associated with <u>pain</u>, <u>death</u> and <u>punishment</u> shows that they are <u>hurt</u> by what happened.

4) **LANGUAGE ABOUT LIFELESSNESS** — The '<u>neutral</u>' tone shows the <u>lack of love</u> between the narrator and their lover, and the <u>pessimistic</u> way the narrator now feels about love in general. The <u>death</u> of their relationship and this <u>lack of hope</u> are reflected in the landscape — it's <u>bleak</u>, <u>decaying</u> and <u>cold</u>.

Remember the feelings and attitudes in the poem

1) **BITTERNESS** — The narrator feels <u>bitter</u> about the <u>breakdown</u> of their relationship — they <u>resent</u> the <u>lack</u> of real <u>emotion</u> behind their lover's smile and the way the lover seemed <u>bored</u>.

2) **PESSIMISM** — Other negative experiences of love since the relationship described in the poem have only <u>confirmed</u> the narrator's pessimistic view of love. The <u>bleak</u> mood and <u>colourless</u> setting show that there's a <u>lack of hope</u> everywhere, even in <u>nature</u>.

Go a step further and give a personal response

Have a go at <u>answering</u> these <u>questions</u> to help you come up with <u>your own ideas</u> about the poem:

Q1. Do you think the narrator blames their lover for the end of their relationship? Why / Why not?

Q2. How is time used in the poem?

Q3. What do you think the title of the poem refers to?

Negative emotions, romantic love, memory...

The tone of bitterness in the poem could be compared with the negative emotions in 'Love's Dog'. You could write about 'One Flesh' if you're looking at how romantic love and feelings can change over time.

Sonnet 43

Enjambment emphasises the speaker's passion — it suggests she is overflowing with love.

This is a different side to her love — it's a calm, constant part of everyday life too.

She loves him effortlessly — it's very natural to her.

Anaphora shows the strength of her feelings. It also emphasises the different words that follow ("freely", "purely") which describe her love.

Question makes the poem's theme clear from the start.

Addresses the object of her love as "thee" — it's direct and personal. However, the lack of a name or gender makes the poem seem universal.

The poem 'counts' each of these ways as it progresses. Makes the speaker sound methodical and intense.

Shows the scale of her love. Repetition of "and" reflects her excitement and passion.

Capitals suggest these words are being used in a spiritual sense. The speaker's love is so deep it's like the desire to understand existence and get close to God. This would have resonated strongly with readers in the 19th century, when society was more religious.

She loves him as willingly as people who always try to do the right thing, and as purely as modest people who turn away from being praised. The link to virtuous conduct suggests her love is morally right.

How do I love thee? Let me count the ways! –
I love thee to the depth and breadth and height
My soul can reach, when feeling out of sight
For the ends of Being and Ideal Grace.
5   I love thee to the level of everyday's
Most quiet need, by sun and candlelight –
I love thee freely, as men strive for Right, –
I love thee purely, as they turn from Praise;
I love thee with the passion, put to use
10 In my old griefs, ... and with my childhood's faith:
I love thee with the love I seemed to lose
With my lost Saints, – I love thee with the breath,
Smiles, tears, of all my life! – and, if God choose,
I shall but love thee better after death.

Mixture of positive and negative emotions shows that she loves him with everything she has — it all links back to her love for him.

She loves him with the passion that religion gave her as a child. This could suggest that her lover has replaced her faith — she almost idolises him.

Their love is presented as eternal as it will outlive their time on earth. The speaker's hope that God supports their love suggests that she believes in its purity.

Caesurae break up the rhythm and make her sound breathless with excitement.

POEM DICTIONARY
Grace — in Christianity, the love and mercy given by God to those who believe in him.

Elizabeth Barrett Browning

Elizabeth Barrett Browning was born in County Durham. She wrote this poem as part of a series of sonnets published in 1850 about her future husband, Robert Browning, called *Sonnets from the Portuguese*.

You've got to know what the poem's about

1) The speaker expresses her <u>intense love</u> for her lover, counting all the <u>different ways</u> in which she loves him.

2) She loves him so <u>deeply</u> that she sees their love as <u>spiritual</u> and <u>sacred</u>.

3) Her love is so <u>great</u> that she believes she will love him even <u>after death</u>.

"How do I love brie? Let me count the ways..."

Learn about the form, structure and language

1) **FORM** — Barrett Browning follows <u>tradition</u> by writing her <u>love poem</u> in the form of a <u>Petrarchan sonnet</u>. This means it conforms to a <u>specific rhyme scheme</u>. It is written in <u>iambic pentameter</u>, and therefore mirrors the rhythm of <u>normal speech</u>, but the metre is disrupted by <u>pauses</u> and <u>repetition</u>, making the speaker sound <u>passionate</u>. The use of the <u>first person</u> also gives the poem a <u>personal</u> feel.

2) **STRUCTURE** — The poem is made up of a series of <u>different ways</u> of <u>defining</u> the speaker's love. The <u>octave</u> (the first eight lines) introduces the poem's main <u>theme</u> — the idea that her love is so intense, it is almost divine. The <u>sestet</u> (the remaining six lines) then develops this theme by showing that she loves him with the <u>emotions</u> of an <u>entire lifetime</u> — from <u>childhood</u> through to, and past, <u>death</u>.

3) **EXAGGERATED LANGUAGE** — The poem uses <u>hyperbole</u> to show the <u>strength</u> of the speaker's feelings. She uses <u>exaggeration</u> as she attempts to put her <u>feelings into words</u> — she is keen to emphasise both the <u>scale</u> of her love and the fact that the <u>experiences</u> of her whole life contribute to its <u>strength</u>.

4) **RELIGIOUS LANGUAGE** — The speaker's love is like a <u>religion</u> to her — it touches <u>all aspects</u> of her life and gives <u>meaning</u> to her existence. Her love is <u>unconditional</u>, like religious faith.

5) **REPETITION** — Using the same words repeatedly at the start of consecutive lines is called <u>anaphora</u>. It emphasises the <u>strength</u> of her feelings — it's as if words can't convey the <u>intensity</u> of her emotions, so she just has to keep repeating the <u>same ones</u> to express the <u>depth</u> of her love.

Remember the feelings and attitudes in the poem

1) **DEEP AND LASTING LOVE** — The speaker uses descriptions of <u>spiritual love</u> to emphasise the <u>strength</u> of her own feelings. The <u>final line</u> also implies that her love is <u>everlasting</u>.

2) **UNSELFISH LOVE** — The speaker asks for <u>nothing in return</u>. She compares herself to people who try to do the <u>right thing</u> without expecting a <u>reward</u>.

3) **VIRTUE** — She considers her love to be <u>morally</u> and <u>spiritually right</u> and worthy of <u>God's support</u>.

Go a step further and give a personal response

Have a go at <u>answering</u> these <u>questions</u> to help you come up with <u>your own ideas</u> about the poem:

Q1.	Why do you think the speaker hopes that her love is supported by God?
Q2.	What is the effect of the rhyme of "breath" and "death" in lines 12 and 14?
Q3.	The speaker focuses only on the positives of love in this poem. What is the effect of this?

Desire and longing, romantic love, adoration...

Compare the speaker's desire in this poem to the desire of the speaker in 'i wanna be yours'. You could also explore how romantic love is presented in this poem compared to the less traditional 'Valentine'.

My Last Duchess

Context — Duke Alfonso II
of Ferrara
Ferrara is a region of Italy. In 1561, the Duke of Ferrara's wife, Lucrezia, died in suspicious circumstances — there were rumours she was poisoned. This story probably inspired Browning to write the poem.

Ferrara

That's my last duchess painted on the wall,
Looking as if she were alive. I call
That piece a wonder, now: Frà Pandolf's hands
Worked busily a day, and there she stands.
5 Will't please you sit and look at her? I said
'Frà Pandolf' by design, for never read
Strangers like you that pictured countenance,
The depth and passion of its earnest glance,
But to myself they turned (since none puts by
10 The curtain I have drawn for you, but I)
And seemed as they would ask me, if they durst
How such a glance came there; so, not the first
Are you to turn and ask thus. Sir, 'twas not
Her husband's presence only, called that spot
15 Of joy into the Duchess' cheek: perhaps
Frà Pandolf chanced to say 'Her mantle laps
Over my lady's wrist too much,' or 'Paint
Must never hope to reproduce the faint
Half-flush that dies along her throat': such stuff
20 Was courtesy, she thought, and cause enough
For calling up that spot of joy. She had
A heart – how shall I say? – too soon made glad,
Too easily impressed; she liked whate'er
She looked on, and her looks went everywhere.
25 Sir, 'twas all one! My favour at her breast,
The dropping of the daylight in the West,
The bough of cherries some officious fool
Broke in the orchard for her, the white mule
She rode with round the terrace – all and each
30 Would draw from her alike the approving speech,
Or blush, at least. She thanked men – good! but thanked
Somehow – I know not how – as if she ranked
My gift of a nine-hundred-years-old name
With anybody's gift. Who'd stoop to blame
35 This sort of trifling? Even had you skill
In speech – which I have not – to make your will
Quite clear to such a one, and say, 'Just this
Or that in you disgusts me; here you miss,
Or there exceed the mark' – and if she let
40 Herself be lessoned so, nor plainly set
Her wits to yours, forsooth, and made excuse,
– E'en then would be some stooping; and I choose
Never to stoop. Oh sir, she smiled, no doubt,
Whene'er I passed her; but who passed without
45 Much the same smile? This grew; I gave commands;
Then all smiles stopped together. There she stands
As if alive. Will't please you rise? We'll meet
The company below, then. I repeat,
The Count your master's known munificence
50 Is ample warrant that no just pretense
Of mine for dowry will be disallowed;
Though his fair daughter's self, as I avowed
At starting, is my object. Nay, we'll go
Together down, sir. Notice Neptune, though,
55 Taming a sea-horse, thought a rarity,
Which Claus of Innsbruck cast in bronze for me!

Annotations (left):
- Sounds polite, but is really quite forceful.
- He controls who looks at the painting, but he couldn't control who looked at his wife when she was alive.
- Reference to death is out of place and suspicious — it hints at the Duchess's fate.
- The Duke struggles to express his irritation.
- She was cheery and friendly — but the Duke means this as a criticism.
- He sounds as if he's justifying himself — he's defensive.
- Repetition of "stoop" in lines 34, 42 and 43 hints at how the Duke felt his wife was beneath him.
- False modesty — he's clearly very skilled at speaking.
- This word suggests he was more concerned about the Duchess's behaviour than he's letting on.
- This seems to be a euphemism for his wife's murder. "I gave commands" is cold and cynical.
- He's arranging his next marriage — his 'Next Duchess'.
- He returns to the subject of his art collection, which emphasises his power and wealth. The story of his last Duchess is a subtle warning to his visitor about how he expects his next wife to behave.

Annotations (right):
- Sounds as if he owns the Duchess herself, not just the picture of her.
- Sets a sinister tone.
- The name of the artist.
- The punctuation doesn't end the line, with the Duke speaking again immediately — he doesn't give his visitor a chance to speak.
- Suggests people were scared of his temper.
- Creates the impression of a question from the visitor, but we hear it through the Duke — he's in complete control.
- Repeating this shows that his wife's blushes bother him.
- The Duke believes that she flirted a lot.
- Enjambment makes it sound as if he's getting carried away by his anger.
- The punctuation and repetition here creates a stuttering effect, which underlines his exasperation with her behaviour.
- He's proud of his history, his important family and the titles of "Duke" and "Duchess".
- The Duke is so proud that even criticising his wife would have been beneath him — he believes she shouldn't need to be reminded how to behave.
- He sounds suspicious of her — maybe he thought she was being unfaithful.

POEM DICTIONARY
countenance — face
durst — dared
mantle — cloak
bough — branch
officious — interfering
forsooth — indeed
munificence — generosity
dowry — money paid to a man by his bride's family when they marry
avowed — said
Neptune — Roman god of the sea

Section One — The Poems

Robert Browning

Browning was born in England but lived in Italy for many years. He was fascinated by the Italian Renaissance (14th-16th centuries) — a period in which the arts flourished. 'My Last Duchess' was published in 1842.

You've got to know what the poem's about

1) The Duke proudly points out the portrait of the Duchess (his former wife) to a visitor.

2) The Duke was angered by the Duchess's behaviour — she was friendly towards everyone and he was annoyed that she treated him just like anyone else.

3) He acted to stop the Duchess's flirtatious behaviour, but he doesn't say how he did this. There are strong hints that he had her murdered.

4) The Duke and his guest walk away from the painting and the reader discovers that the Duke's visitor has come to arrange the Duke's next marriage.

Learn about the form, structure and language

1) **FORM** — The poem is a dramatic monologue written in iambic pentameter. This reinforces the impression that the Duke is in conversation with his visitor. The rhyming couplets show the Duke's desire for control, but the enjambment suggests that he gets carried away with his anger and passions. This creates a picture of a somewhat unstable character, whose obsession with power is unsettling.

2) **STRUCTURE** — The poem is framed by the visit to the Duke's gallery, but the Duke gets caught up in talking about the Duchess instead of describing the art. The poem builds towards a kind of confession, before the identity of the visitor is revealed, and the Duke moves on to talking about another artwork.

3) **POWER AND OBJECTIFICATION** — The Duke wanted to have power and control over the Duchess. He saw her as another of his possessions, to be collected and admired, just like his expensive artworks.

4) **DRAMATIC IRONY** — The things the Duke says about the Duchess seem quite innocent, but they often have more sinister meanings for the reader. There's a gap between what the Duke tells his listener, and what the poet allows us to read between the lines.

5) **STATUS** — Status is really important to the Duke. He cares about how others see him.

Remember the feelings and attitudes in the poem

1) **PRIDE** — The Duke is very proud of his possessions and his status.

2) **JEALOUSY** — He couldn't stand that the Duchess treated him the same as everyone else (lines 31-34).

3) **POWER** — The Duke enjoys the control he has over the painting (lines 9-10). He didn't have this power over the Duchess when she was alive.

Go a step further and give a personal response

Have a go at answering these questions to help you come up with your own ideas about the poem:

Q1.   Do you think the Duke ever had any affection for the Duchess? Why / Why not?

Q2.   How is the Duke's view of himself different from the way the reader sees him?

Q3.   Is the title of the poem effective? Why? Can you think of a suitable alternative title?

Q4.   Why do you think the Duke is the only one who speaks in the poem?

KEY THEMES

Romantic love, desire and longing, death...

You could compare the Duke's obsessive desire for control over the Duchess to the speaker's intense desire in 'i wanna be yours'. The dangerous side of romantic love is also hinted at in 'Valentine'.

16

First Date – She   First Date – He

First Date — She

Suggests strong emotions and attraction — she is excited to be on the date.

Repetition of the first line sounds as though she's revisiting what she said and questioning it — perhaps with a sense of regret.

First lines mirror each other, which immediately creates a strong link between the two poems. The speakers are both looking back and trying to work out how they ended up in this situation.

He thinks she is "totally lost in" the music, i.e. very interested in it, but she's more likely to just be "lost", as she doesn't really have an interest in classical music.

Irony — the concert isn't "suitable" for either of them as they don't like classical music, nor is it suitable as a first date because they can't talk to each other.

Both narrators were vague about their likes / dislikes — they both told half-truths to try to find common ground.

First Date — She

I said I liked classical music.
It wasn't exactly a lie.
I hoped he would get the impression
That my brow was acceptably high.

5   I said I liked classical music.
I mentioned Vivaldi and Bach.
And he asked me along to this concert.
Here we are, sitting in the half-dark.

I was thrilled to be asked to the concert.
10   I couldn't decide what to wear.
I hope I look tastefully sexy.
I've done what I can with my hair.

Yes, I'm thrilled to be here at this concert.
I couldn't care less what they play
15   But I'm trying my hardest to listen
So I'll have something clever to say.

When I glance at his face it's a picture
Of rapt concentration. I see
He is totally into this music
20   And quite undistracted by me.

The "half-dark" represents their state of misunderstanding.

The tense changes in the second stanza of each poem, bringing the reader into the present situation.

Repetition of "thrilled" could emphasise how pleased she is, but could also be an attempt to convince herself that she is excited to be there.

First Date — He

She said she liked classical music.
I implied I was keen on it too.
Though I don't often go to a concert,
It wasn't entirely untrue.

5   I looked for a suitable concert
And here we are, on our first date.
The traffic was dreadful this evening
And I arrived ten minutes late.

So we haven't had much time for talking
10   And I'm a bit nervous. I see
She is totally lost in the music
And quite undistracted by me.

In that dress she is very attractive –
The neckline can't fail to intrigue.
15   I mustn't appear too besotted.
Perhaps she is out of my league.

Where are we? I glance at the programme
But I've put my glasses away.
I'd better start paying attention
20   Or else I'll have nothing to say.

The caesura creates an unnatural pause in the line which mirrors the awkwardness he feels.

Rhetorical question not only refers to the concert, but also to their relationship and whether it has a future.

He is distracted by her beauty — the opposite of what she thinks is happening.

She feels inadequate and worries that her date is intellectually superior to her. This mirrors his feelings of inadequacy ("Perhaps she is out of my league").

This is an example of dramatic irony. The reader is given an insight into both perspectives and can see how they both misinterpret the situation in the same way — neither of them really see what's going on.

The word "tastefully" shows her attempt to dress for the occasion. She wants to impress her date but not look out of place at the concert.

He is concerned about what will happen when the concert ends — he is keen to impress her, which is similar to her concerns that she should have "something clever to say."

"When he said Chopin, I thought he meant a cookery class."

POEM DICTIONARY
(high)brow — intellectual or with good taste
Vivaldi and Bach — famous classical composers
rapt — fascinated
besotted — infatuated or in love with

Wendy Cope

Wendy Cope is an English poet who's known for her humour. These poems were published in 2012 as part of a collection called *Family Values* — a series of poems looking at different people at the same concert.

You've got to know what the poems are about

1) The two poems describe a <u>first date</u> from two <u>different perspectives</u> — one <u>male</u>, one <u>female</u>.

2) Both speakers told <u>half-truths</u> in an <u>attempt to impress</u> each other and are now at a classical music <u>concert</u> that <u>neither</u> of them would normally have <u>chosen</u> to go to.

3) While trying to impress one another, they each wrongly believe that the other is <u>not interested</u> in them.

Learn about the form, structure and language

1) **FORM** — The poems are a pair of <u>monologues</u> with <u>ABCB</u> rhyme schemes. This keeps the tone of each poem <u>light</u> and <u>humorous</u>, and the separation of the <u>rhyming lines</u> mirrors the <u>distance</u> between the couple. Both poems have <u>regular line and stanza</u> lengths — this precision could reflect the <u>overly analytical</u> thought processes of each speaker — they each seem to be over-thinking the situation.

2) **STRUCTURE** — The two poems <u>mirror</u> each other, both on the <u>page</u> and in <u>subject matter</u>. Each speaker gives <u>brief summary</u> of <u>why</u> they are at the concert, talks about their <u>experience</u> of the concert and then touches on the relationship's <u>prospects</u>. The <u>similarities</u> between the <u>poems</u> suggest <u>similarities</u> between the <u>speakers</u>.

3) **REPETITION** — The speakers use lots of the <u>same words</u> and <u>phrases</u>. This creates an <u>echo</u> effect, and shows how well-matched the couple are, <u>despite</u> their <u>concerns</u>. The poems tell <u>two sides</u> of the <u>same story</u> — they could <u>subconsciously</u> be <u>imitating</u> the other through <u>nerves</u> and the desire to be liked.

4) **LANGUAGE ABOUT MISUNDERSTANDING** — Phrases like "It wasn't exactly a lie" and "It wasn't entirely untrue" show how the speakers have <u>misled</u> each other. They continue to misunderstand each other in the concert hall — they both believe that the other person is "<u>lost in</u>" or "<u>totally into</u>" the music, but the poems show that they are actually <u>thinking</u> about <u>each other</u>.

5) **IRONY** — <u>Dramatic irony</u> (when the reader knows something the characters don't) is used to <u>humorous effect</u>. The <u>divide</u> between <u>appearance</u> and <u>reality</u> is <u>clear</u> to the reader, who sees both sides of the story.

Remember the feelings and attitudes in the poems

1) **NERVOUSNESS** — The couple are both <u>nervous</u> and <u>self-conscious</u>. They feel as though they need to <u>impress</u> each other and <u>worry</u> that they aren't good enough for one another.

2) **ATTRACTION** — The <u>attraction</u> between the pair is <u>clear</u> — she feels "thrilled" and he is "besotted" — but it is <u>unclear</u> if they will be able to <u>overcome</u> the <u>misunderstandings</u> between them.

Go a step further and give a personal response

Have a go at <u>answering</u> these <u>questions</u> to help you come up with <u>your own ideas</u> about the poems:

Q1.   Why do you think the poet uses "She" and "He" in the titles rather than their names?

Q2.   How do you think the speakers feel about each other? Use examples to justify your answer.

Q3.   Do you think the poems are about a young couple or an older couple? Explain your answer.

Romantic love, desire and longing, distance...

You can compare the lovers' first impressions in this poem to the knight and the lady in 'La Belle Dame Sans Merci'. Look at how the complexities of romantic love are presented in comparison to 'One Flesh'.

Valentine

Immediately clear that this is not a traditional love poem.

Personal pronouns highlight that this poem is for a specific person.

Stereotypical symbols of love. The speaker implies these are clichéd and lack meaning.

Introduces the gift of an onion, which becomes an extended metaphor for love. It's an unexpected contrast with the first line.

The moon is a traditional symbol of love and fertility.

The use of "It" makes it unclear whether the speaker means the onion or love itself.

The onion symbolises the way love can cause pain. Language like "blind" and "grief" is strongly negative, unlike traditional Valentine's Day messages.

Alliteration makes these seem overly sentimental and makes the narrator seem disdainful of them.

Echoes the wedding vow "For as long as we both shall live".

The offer of an onion in line 6 changes to a command. The speaker could be merely encouraging their lover to accept the gift, or their tone may be interpreted as confrontational, which makes the mood darker.

By placing "Lethal" alone on an end-stopped line, the speaker emphasises the idea that the onion symbolises danger and death. This is shocking and unexpected in a love poem.

This emphasises that the onion is a plain, unsentimental gift.

Hints at sexual love and physical intimacy.

Enjambment breaks these similes up, making the poem feel disjointed. The separation also emphasises how unpredictable the similes are — the comparisons don't necessarily end in the way the reader expects.

This line is unconnected to any others and almost divides the poem in two. It could represent the 'heart' of the poem — the speaker is trying to find the true meaning of love.

This repeated line presents the speaker as insistent and forceful, establishing a sense of unease.

Love is described in physical terms. There's also a suggestion that it can be dangerous and possessive.

Reference to a wedding ring could be a proposal. It's undermined by the sense of hesitation in the next line.

The repetition of "cling" on two separate lines emphasises the inescapability of its "scent". The word also has a dark double meaning — it hints that love can be possessive and suffocating.

A powerful, disturbing final image. There's a hint that it refers to something more sinister than chopping an onion — but exactly what it could be is left unsaid. It implies that love has the power to wound.

Not a red rose or a satin heart.

I give you an onion.
It is a moon wrapped in brown paper.
It promises light
5   like the careful undressing of love.

Here.
It will blind you with tears
like a lover.
It will make your reflection
10   a wobbling photo of grief.

I am trying to be truthful.

Not a cute card or a kissogram.

I give you an onion.
Its fierce kiss will stay on your lips,
15   possessive and faithful
as we are,
for as long as we are.

Take it.
Its platinum loops shrink to a wedding-ring,
20   if you like.
Lethal.
Its scent will cling to your fingers,
cling to your knife.

Carol Ann Duffy

Carol Ann Duffy is a Scottish poet who, in 2009, became the first woman to hold the post of Poet Laureate in the UK. 'Valentine' was originally published in 1993 as part of Duffy's collection, *Mean Time*.

You've got to know what the poem's about

1) The speaker of the poem is giving a <u>gift</u> to their partner. Rather than a <u>traditional</u> Valentine's gift, their gift is an <u>onion</u>.

2) The rest of the poem explains why the onion is a more <u>appropriate symbol</u> of love than other stereotypical gifts.

"What kind of chocolates did he get you?"
"Um, the onion kind..."

Learn about the form, structure and language

1) **FORM** — Duffy's poem is very <u>different</u> to traditional love poems. For instance, it is written in stanzas of <u>irregular lengths</u>, several of only one line, which makes the poem seem <u>disjointed</u>. Some lines are made up of <u>single words</u>, which gives emphasis to the <u>forceful</u> tone of the speaker.

2) **STRUCTURE** — The poem is a <u>list</u> of the ways the onion symbolises love. Words and ideas are <u>built up</u> and <u>repeated</u> throughout the poem. This could mirror the <u>different layers</u> of an onion, as the poem's meaning is revealed <u>gradually</u>. The tone is initially quite <u>playful</u>, but the speaker's <u>repeated insistence</u> that their partner accepts their gift could be read as either <u>encouraging</u> or <u>confrontational</u>.

3) **EXTENDED METAPHOR** — The extended metaphor of the onion is used to <u>represent love</u>. The speaker sees the onion as an <u>honest symbol</u> — it symbolises the <u>joy</u> and <u>intimacy</u> of love, but also the <u>pain</u>. It's an <u>unusual metaphor</u>, which contrasts with more <u>stereotypical</u> romantic symbols, like roses and cards.

4) **DIRECT ADDRESS** — The poem is written in the <u>first person</u> and <u>directly</u> addresses an unknown partner as "you" — it's very <u>personal</u>. The speaker uses <u>commands</u> like "Take it", which may be seen as <u>forceful</u>.

5) **DANGEROUS LANGUAGE** — There's an unusual amount of <u>negative language</u> for a love poem. Words like "blind", "fierce" and "Lethal" have a <u>dark undertone</u>. The speaker implies that this is a <u>possessive</u> relationship, while the word "knife" at the end hints that it might be <u>dangerous</u>.

Remember the feelings and attitudes in the poem

1) **LOVE** — The poet explores <u>different forms</u> of love. Love can be <u>physical</u> or <u>emotional</u>. It can be "fierce" and <u>possessive</u>, and cause <u>pain</u>. There are also references to <u>marriage</u> and being <u>faithful</u>.

2) **HONESTY** — Above all, the speaker takes <u>pride</u> in being <u>honest</u> about love. They suggest that the <u>traditional</u> images of love, like red roses and cute cards, <u>don't</u> say anything <u>real</u> about love.

3) **DANGER** — At the end of the poem, there's a growing sense of <u>danger</u>, although it's only <u>implied</u>.

Go a step further and give a personal response

Have a go at <u>answering</u> these <u>questions</u> to help you come up with <u>your own ideas</u> about the poem:

Q1. What does the word "platinum" (line 19) suggest about the onion?

Q2. Do you think the poem describes a happy relationship? Explain your answer.

Q3. How do you feel at the end of the poem? What do you think will happen next?

KEY THEMES

Romantic love, death and suffering...

Think about the unusual aspects of this poem and compare it with a more conventional portrayal of love, such as in 'Sonnet 43'. 'My Last Duchess' also presents romantic love as having an element of danger.

One Flesh

The title is a quote from the Bible about marriage — "and the two will become one flesh" (Mark 10:8). This signifies the deep connection between two individuals who come together as a married couple. The title hints that the poem will explore the idea of marriage in some way.

Opening line creates a picture of separation. "now" indicates that this is a change, but the pause created by the caesura hints that the separation is already quite pronounced.

Simile hints that she is mourning the passing of time.

Subject pronouns start consecutive lines — this reinforces the couple's separation and emphasises their separate activities.

Shipwreck imagery suggests that they have no control over their situation.

Present tense description gives a sense of stillness, emphasising that the couple seem to be waiting for something.

Suggests that they feel guilty, and that they are struggling to express their feelings in words.

There is a clear contrast between their current "cool" relationship and the heat of the "passion" and "fire" (line 18) they used to feel.

Placement of "Chastity" at the start of the line increases its force. The way it "faces them" suggests that it is something negative to be feared.

A bleak description — their lives up to this point have simply been to prepare for this separation.

Repetition emphasises the contradiction of the couple being both "apart" and "close together" — "strangely" suggests the speaker find this difficult to understand.

Physical passion is not necessarily the only indication of intimacy. The speaker offers the possibility that the couple are still close despite their lack of physical intimacy.

Simile shows that there is still a connection between them but it is thin and weak, like thread. They hold onto it but do not use it to get any closer together.

Feather metaphor indicates that time has passed by so gently and changed them so quietly that they may not even have noticed it happening.

The speaker reveals that they are talking about their own parents. This makes the poem seem more personal and gives context for the reflective tone.

Poem ends on an uncertain note — perhaps to reflect the speaker's uncertainty about how much the relationship has actually cooled, as well as questioning if the parents are aware of how much has changed.

The final lines of the poem are reflective — the speaker wonders if their parents are aware of the changes that have occurred over time.

Lying apart now, each in a separate bed,
He with a book, keeping the light on late,
She like a girl dreaming of childhood,
All men elsewhere – it is as if they wait
5 Some new event: the book he holds unread,
Her eyes fixed on the shadows overhead.

Tossed up like flotsam from a former passion,
How cool they lie. They hardly ever touch,
10 Or if they do it is like a confession
Of having little feeling – or too much.
Chastity faces them, a destination
For which their whole lives were a preparation.

Strangely apart, yet strangely close together,
15 Silence between them like a thread to hold
And not wind in. And time itself's a feather
Touching them gently. Do they know they're old,
These two who are my father and my mother
Whose fire from which I came, has now grown cold?

Context — The Movement
Elizabeth Jennings is often associated with a group of poets called 'The Movement.' These poets believed that poetry should be simple and traditional in its form and content, in contrast to modernism, a style which experimented with form and rejected realism. 'One Flesh' is a good example of this, with its straightforward rhyme scheme, conventional form and relatable subject matter.

POEM DICTIONARY
flotsam — wreckage or debris from a shipwreck
confession — a formal admission of guilt
Chastity — total restraint from sexual pleasures

Elizabeth Jennings

Elizabeth Jennings published 'One Flesh' in 1966. She was a devoted Catholic, which may have influenced her poems. Despite their personal tone, she insisted that her poems should not be read as autobiographical.

You've got to know what the poem's about

1) The poem describes the relationship between the speaker's parents in its later years.

2) It centres around the changes that have happened to them — it describes their physical separation and considers their lack of sexual intimacy, in contrast to how their relationship used to be.

3) The poem appears to explore the sadness of a marriage that has lost its intimacy, but it could also be about how a bond remains between a couple even when physical affection has been lost.

Learn about the form, structure and language

1) **FORM** — The first two stanzas of the poem end with rhyming couplets, which could signify the underlying unity between the couple. The final stanza is different — the last two lines continue the ABAB rhyme scheme in the rest of the stanza. The disappearance of the couplet reinforces the separation between the couple, as the rhyming lines are separated. The rhythm of the poem is steady, hinting at the monotony of their relationship.

2) **STRUCTURE** — The speaker discusses the couple's day-to-day separation, then focuses on their emotional separation. The final verse is reflective, as the speaker wonders if any connection remains.

3) **RELIGIOUS LANGUAGE** — The use of religious language, e.g. "confession", could hint that the couple's spiritual connection remains despite their physical separation, or that they have stayed faithful to their Christian marriage vows despite their dwindling passion.

4) **IMAGERY** — Metaphors and similes, e.g. "time itself's a feather", are used to explore the differences between the past and present and between the husband and wife. Imagery shows how the speaker is trying to find ways to understand and explain the changes they have seen in their parents' relationship.

Remember the feelings and attitudes in the poem

1) **DISTANCE** — The couple in the poem seem detached from each other, but the distance between them may just be physical — an emotional connection may still exist between them.

2) **RESIGNATION** — The speaker's parents seem passive in their acceptance of their situation. It is perhaps that they have resigned themselves to the change, knowing that they cannot alter the passage of time.

Go a step further and give a personal response

Have a go at answering these questions to help you come up with your own ideas about the poem:

Q1.   Do you think the couple regret the lack of physical contact? Explain your answer.
Q2.   Find two different examples of caesurae in the poem. What effect do they have?
Q3.   Why do you think the speaker does not reveal their identity until the final couplet?

Distance, negative emotions, romantic love...

'First Date – She / First Date – He' also show a pair who feel separated, although they do try to connect with each other. The negative effects of growing older are also seen in 'A Child to his Sick Grandfather'.

i wanna be yours

Unusual metaphors show the poem is a different type of love poetry, without clichéd images.

The poem starts with an imperative, but it's a gentle, almost respectful demand, giving the power to the other person.

Using a mundane object in the opening metaphor amuses the reader and sets a light-hearted tone.

The speaker is willing to give up their independence to please the other person. "you call" is emphatic, showing the strength of their desire

Speaker is promising to be reliable, and "never" indicates that their feelings will last forever.

The stanza is concluded with a repetition of the title — the speaker's ultimate aim.

The speaker knows that life often has difficult moments that can make us sad — they want to shield the other person from them.

A more forceful imperative — shows how strong the speaker's desire is.

Contrast between the "raincoat", which symbolises the mundane reality of life, and the "dreamboat", which suggests idealised, romantic ideas. The speaker has thought about all the different aspects of life and love and wants to be there through all of it.

Slang suggests that the speaker isn't trying to hide behind fancy language — they are confident that their declaration of love is enough.

The speaker uses simple language to reflect how their feelings are straightforward.

Repetition of "let me" reinforces the strength of the speaker's desire, but could also hint at their desperation.

The speaker wants to offer comfort and protection. Image suggests intimacy — the speaker wants to be physically close to the other person.

The speaker wants to be useful, like a heater — they see love as more than words and romantic gestures.

The speaker's vow refers to an electric meter running out of power, but this also sounds like a traditional romantic promise — this emphasises the romance and affection behind the mundane imagery.

They want their presence to be missed when they are not around, and to be as important as warmth. Suggests the speaker wants to feel needed.

Repetition of "deep" is emphatic, and the simile shows their love to be powerful and vast.

Repetition is lyrical but almost comical. It could be an attempt to mock traditional love songs where words are repeated so much they lose meaning.

Repetition of "i wanna be yours" at the end of each stanza emphasises the constancy of the speaker's love and devotion.

First mention of a third person — "hers" seems specific, as if the speaker is talking about someone in particular. It could be that the person they are addressing has questioned their commitment and the speaker is trying to convince them of their devotion.

let me be your vacuum cleaner
breathing in your dust
let me be your ford cortina
i will never rust
5 if you like your coffee hot
let me be your coffee pot
you call the shots
i wanna be yours

let me be your raincoat
10 for those frequent rainy days
let me be your dreamboat
when you wanna sail away
let me be your teddy bear
take me with you anywhere
15 i don't care
i wanna be yours

let me be your electric meter
i will not run out
let me be the electric heater
20 you get cold without
let me be your setting lotion
hold your hair
with deep devotion
deep as the deep
25 atlantic ocean
that's how deep is my emotion
deep deep deep deep de deep deep
i don't wanna be hers
i wanna be yours

POEM DICTIONARY
Ford Cortina — a popular car in the 1970s
electric meter — a device that measures electricity usage,
often needing to be paid into so the power does not run out
setting lotion — lotion applied to damp hair to help keep it
in place for longer once styled

Section One — The Poems

John Cooper Clarke

John Cooper Clarke is a punk poet who became famous for his humorous poetry, which is often performed on stage. 'i wanna be yours' was released in 1982, as part of a spoken word album that had backing music.

You've got to know what the poem's about

1) The speaker is <u>telling</u> someone how much they <u>care</u> for them.

2) They talk about all the things they want to <u>do</u> and <u>be</u> for them, using <u>everyday objects</u> to convey their <u>desire</u>.

3) The <u>status</u> of the speaker's <u>relationship</u> with the addressee is <u>ambiguous</u> — the poem could be about <u>convincing</u> a <u>current lover</u> of their <u>devotion</u> or about the speaker's <u>desire</u> to be with <u>someone new</u>.

"Thanks, but I like my coffee cold, and I'm afraid raincoat applications closed last week."

Learn about the form, structure and language

1) **FORM** — The poem has a <u>mostly regular</u> rhyme scheme and rhythm, which gives the poem a <u>lyrical</u> quality. It is <u>unconventional</u> though, with <u>no punctuation</u> or <u>capitalisation</u>. This could show how the speaker's <u>love</u> can't be fully <u>constrained</u> by <u>tradition</u> or <u>rules</u>, emphasising the <u>intensity</u> of the speaker's feelings. The <u>third stanza</u> is <u>longer</u> and <u>departs</u> from the regular rhyme scheme, perhaps indicating that the speaker is getting <u>carried away</u> with their emotions.

2) **STRUCTURE** — The poem is made up of a <u>sequence of images</u> which the speaker uses to explain their feelings. The <u>third stanza</u> departs from this <u>sequence</u> of images, emphasising the speaker's increasingly <u>intense emotions</u>.

3) **SIMPLE LANGUAGE** — The speaker's frequent use of <u>monosyllabic</u>, <u>informal</u> language and <u>slang</u> to describe their feelings and desires makes them seem <u>straightforward</u> and <u>honest</u>.

4) **EVERYDAY IMAGERY** — The speaker <u>rejects</u> traditional, clichéd imagery and instead uses imagery of <u>everyday objects</u>. This seems more <u>genuine</u> but also <u>creates humour</u>, which could <u>raise questions</u> over how serious the speaker is being.

5) **REPETITION** — Repetition of phrases such as "<u>let me</u>" and "<u>i wanna be yours</u>" highlights the <u>depth</u> of the speaker's <u>emotion</u>, but also gives the <u>impression</u> that the speaker is <u>pleading</u> with the other person.

Remember the feelings and attitudes in the poem

1) DEVOTION — The speaker claims to be utterly <u>devoted</u> to the person they are talking to, and is willing to commit to being a <u>constant</u> and <u>useful</u> part of their life.

2) DESIRE — The speaker <u>longs</u> to <u>belong</u> to the other person. The poem only offers the <u>speaker's point of view</u> though, so there is <u>no indication</u> whether their wishes will be <u>fulfilled</u>.

Go a step further and give a personal response

Have a go at <u>answering</u> these <u>questions</u> to help you come up with <u>your own ideas</u> about the poem:

Q1.   Do you think the speaker sounds obsessive? Explain your answer.

Q2.   How effective do you think the everyday descriptions are in conveying love and desire?

Q3.   Do you think the humour in the poem undermines the speaker's sincerity? Why / why not?

Romantic love, desire and longing, adoration...

'i wanna be yours' uses everyday images to express romantic love, which you could compare to 'Love's Dog' and 'Valentine'. You could also compare the devotion of the speaker in this poem to 'Sonnet 43'.

Love's Dog

First-person "I" makes the poem instantly seem personal and based on experience.

The opening couplet introduces different sides of love — this implies that the poem will be a balanced discussion about the positives and negatives of love.

Unusual use of medical language — portrays love as a disease. Compares the excitement of finding love ("diagnosis") with the fear of long-term commitment ("prognosis").

People in love can be selfish, and love can be overwhelming.

Reference to 'Alice's Adventures in Wonderland' by Lewis Carroll — a story about a young girl's adventures in a fantasy land. A cake that makes Alice grow in size says 'eat me', and a liquid that makes her smaller says 'drink me'. This reference hints that love can be magical and have unexpected consequences.

Two "love" statements in a row — breaks the pattern of previous stanzas. The repetition of "love" is almost hypnotic — love can hypnotise you.

Implies honesty and openness — the speaker seems to value sincerity in a relationship.

Another reference to the 'drink me' potion in 'Alice's Adventures in Wonderland'. Here, it hints at love's ability to make you feel small and vulnerable.

Prolonged extreme heat — implies that love can be unpleasant and potentially painful in the long-term.

Could represent the short bursts of fun and exhilaration love can provide, in contrast to the unpleasant and long "boil-wash".

Couplet has a different structure. "loathe" is more emphatic and alters the tone — the speaker seems more passionate.

What I love about love is its diagnosis
What I hate about love is its prognosis

What I hate about love is its me me me
What I love about love is its Eat-me/Drink-me

5 What I love about love is its petting zoo
What I love about love is its zookeeper – you

What I love about love is its truth serum
What I hate about love is its shrinking potion

What I love about love is its doubloons
10 What I love about love is its bird-bones

What I hate about love is its boil-wash
What I love about love is its spin-cycle

What I loathe about love is its burnt toast and bonemeal
What I hate about love is its bent cigarette

15 What I love about love is its pirate
What I hate about love is its sick parrot

Implies closeness and physical intimacy.

The speaker addresses another person — makes the generalised statements seem more personal.

"zookeeper" cares for and looks after them.

Like gold coins, love is precious and rare.

Birds are crafted for flight — could perhaps indicate how light and carefree love can make people feel.

References to the kitchen and garden could represent the speaker's resentment of domestic monotony. The plosive 'b' sounds indicate frustration with everyday life.

Image of something that has become useless — could hint at loss of libido (sex drive) over time.

Poem ends with hate, which perhaps shows how the initial excitement of being in love can be lost and replaced by negative emotions.

The pirate perhaps represents the speaker's lover, portraying them as exciting and adventurous. The parrot could represent the speaker, who is emotionally and physically tied to the pirate but is "sick" — perhaps overwhelmed by the depth of emotion they feel.

<u>Context — Edwin Morgan</u>
Jen Hadfield wrote 'Love's Dog' in response to Scottish poet Edwin Morgan's 'A View of Things', in which he writes, "what I hate about love is its dog". Dogs are reliable and faithful, so the title could refer to this positive, comforting side of love. Conversely, having a dog is a big commitment, much like the hard work and dedication required to make relationships work — perhaps not something the speaker wants to commit to.

POEM DICTIONARY
diagnosis — identification of an illness or problem
prognosis — the outcome of an illness or problem
truth serum — a drug which makes people tell the truth
doubloons — old Spanish gold coins, associated with pirates
bonemeal — fertiliser made from crushed animal bones

Section One — The Poems

Jen Hadfield

At 30, Jen Hadfield was the youngest ever winner of the T. S. Eliot Poetry Prize. She won it in 2008 for her *Nigh-No-Place* collection which included 'Love's Dog' and was also shortlisted for the Forward Poetry Prize.

You've got to know what the poem's about

1) The poem is about what the speaker loves and hates about being in love. The poem emphasises that relationships are often made up of both emotions.

2) It uses things not traditionally associated with love to explore the variety of emotions it can generate.

3) The speaker doesn't seem to reach a conclusion — the poem is more of a discussion about love.

Learn about the form, structure and language

1) **FORM** — The poem is made up of eight couplets. There is no regular rhyme scheme — some couplets rhyme, some only half rhyme, some do not rhyme at all. This lack of regularity is perhaps symbolic of relationships — sometimes couples are harmonious and sometimes they clash.

2) **STRUCTURE** — Lines mostly alternate between statements about what the speaker loves and hates about love, but there is no set pattern. There are nine 'love' statements in the poem, but only seven 'hate' statements — this could indicate that despite their complaints, their overall opinion is positive.

3) **ANAPHORA** — Anaphora is where a word or phrase is repeated at the start of consecutive sentences or lines. The same phrases are repeated to start most lines in the poem, which adds rhythm and a degree of predictability, but there isn't a strict pattern — like love, it is ultimately unpredictable.

4) **FANTASY IMAGERY** — There are multiple references to fantasy stories in the poem, perhaps suggesting that love is an adventure and can be exciting and unexpected.

5) **DOMESTIC IMAGERY** — Everyday images offset the images of fantasy and adventure and act as a reminder that love isn't always extraordinary — the reality of it can be quite different and ordinary.

6) **SICKNESS IMAGERY** — The speaker seems to view love as an illness — the poem starts with medical imagery and ends with an image of sickness. This imagery could be related to the idea of 'lovesickness' — the speaker does not like the idea that love can overwhelm them like an illness would.

Remember the feelings and attitudes in the poem

1) REALISM — Traditional love poetry tends to idealise love, but the speaker in the poem is more balanced and realistic about the experience. They acknowledge the negative aspects of love as well as the positive, indicating that they've thought about it thoroughly.

2) INDECISIVENESS — The speaker seems torn. The poem could be their attempt to work out whether or not they like being in love, but as they do not reach a conclusion, their opinion remains ambiguous.

Go a step further and give a personal response

Have a go at answering these questions to help you come up with your own ideas about the poem:

Q1. What do you think the overall tone of the poem is?
Q2. What effect does the poem's lack of punctuation have?
Q3. To what extent do the contrasting ideas about love imply that it is a constant struggle?

KEY THEMES

Romantic love, suffering, negative emotions...

Suffering caused by a relationship is also explored in 'My Father Would Not Show Us'. The negativity in the poem could be compared to the narrator's bitterness towards the relationship in 'Neutral Tones'.

Nettles

The nettles are personified — the speaker describes them as trained and malicious soldiers.

Opening words show that the speaker is talking about something personal.

The tone of the poem is reflective here — the speaker is contemplating the irony of the name "nettle bed".

Idea that nettles are threatening is introduced — spears are plant stems but also weapons.

The speaker becomes less personal, perhaps trying to control their emotions.

"watery" suggests that the boy's smile is weak and that he has been crying — he is still hurt, but his parents have made him feel better.

Internal rhyme with the harsh 'k' sounds shows the fierce emotion the parent feels as they prepare the weapon.

Neat alliteration shows parent's pride / pleasure in clearing the entire bed of nettles.

My son aged three fell in the nettle bed.
'Bed' seemed a curious name for those green spears,
That regiment of spite behind the shed:
It was no place for rest. With sobs and tears
5 The boy came seeking comfort and I saw
White blisters beaded on his tender skin.
We soothed him till his pain was not so raw.
At last he offered us a watery grin,
And then I took my billhook, honed the blade
10 And went outside and slashed in fury with it
Till not a nettle in that fierce parade
Stood upright any more. And then I lit
A funeral pyre to burn the fallen dead,
But in two weeks the busy sun and rain
15 Had called up tall recruits behind the shed:
My son would often feel sharp wounds again.

Emotive adjectives emphasise the child's pain and vulnerability.

Contrast between the restrained "honed" and emotive "slashed". The speaker's initial restraint makes their uncontrolled behaviour seem more shocking.

The regular rhythm is broken — "it" adds an extra syllable to the line. This disrupts the steady tempo, showing the raw emotion the parent feels.

"My son" from the first line is repeated here — the son continues to be the parent's focus.

Change of tense — the speaker is also reflecting on painful memories that happened after this incident.

The new nettles are personified as "tall recruits" being called up for active service. The parent's efforts have been in vain as the nettles have grown back.

Imagery of soldiers lost in battle implies that the parent is treating the nettles with respect — perhaps shows that despite their anger, the parent respects the power and force of nature.

It looked like an innocent veg patch, but Barry wasn't fooled — he knew his turnips were preparing for war.

POEM DICTIONARY
regiment — a unit of soldiers in the army
billhook — a garden tool with a sharp blade
honed — sharpened
funeral pyre — a pile of flammable material used in some funeral ceremonies to burn the corpse

Vernon Scannell

Vernon Scannell was a British poet who was in the army in World War Two. He had six children, but two of them died before him. 'Nettles' was published in 1980, and it is believed to be about a personal memory.

You've got to know what the poem's about

1) The speaker (a parent) describes a time when their son fell in a bed of nettles.

2) The son came inside crying and his parents soothed him until he felt better.

3) The speaker then went outside and destroyed the nettle bed, but it grew back two weeks later.

4) The poem ends with the speaker reflecting on the suffering their child has faced since then.

Learn about the form, structure and language

1) **FORM** — The poem is made up of one stanza with an ABAB rhyme scheme. This simple rhyme scheme reflects the everyday subject matter. It is written in iambic pentameter — this creates a steady rhythm which echoes the beat of a marching army, but could also reflect the steady, beating heart of a parent. Enjambment in the poem often shows strong emotions, e.g. in lines 9-13 it suggests the speaker's powerful anger.

2) **STRUCTURE** — The poem is a narrative account of an event, told in chronological order. It starts and ends with a focus on the son, showing that the parent's priority will always be their child. The focus of the final line shifts from the memory of the nettles to other painful experiences in the son's life.

3) **MILITARY IMAGERY** — Throughout the poem, the nettles are compared to an army of soldiers. The imagery reflects the power of nature and also highlights the persistence of the enemy — despite the parent's best efforts to rid the garden of nettles, more grow. The war imagery is in direct contrast to the domestic image of a child playing in the garden, highlighting the child's innocence and vulnerability.

4) **EMOTIVE LANGUAGE** — Emotive language is initially used to show the child's pain, and then goes on to highlight the depth of the parent's feeling. Words like "raw", "tender" and "slashed" are striking, and involve the reader in both the child's pain and the parent's fury.

Remember the feelings and attitudes in the poem

1) **PAIN** — The poem highlights the child's physical pain from the nettle stings and also the parent's emotional pain in reaction to their child being hurt.

2) **ANGER** — The parent's violent reaction against the nettles shows their anger and frustration at the situation, but also the depth of their love for the child.

3) **PROTECTION** — The parent takes revenge on the nettles in an attempt to protect their child from further harm — they perhaps regret that they could not protect them the first time.

Go a step further and give a personal response

Have a go at answering these questions to help you come up with your own ideas about the poem:

Q1. Why do you think Scannell chose to write the poem as one stanza rather than several?

Q2. What emotions or images does the title 'Nettles' make you think of?

Q3. What do you think "sharp wounds" in the final line of the poem might refer to?

Family relationships, suffering, memory...

The parent's reaction to the child's pain could be compared to how the wife in 'The Manhunt' deals with her husband's suffering. A family relationship is also presented in 'A Child to his Sick Grandfather'.

The Manhunt

Repetition of phrases emphasises that the soldier's recovery is slow and painstaking.

The first couplet could be the start of a traditional love poem. It echoes the first stages of a new relationship and suggests the couple are reconnecting.

After the first phase,
after passionate nights and intimate days,

only then would he let me trace
the frozen river which ran through his face,

Image of physical brokenness suggests that her husband struggles to talk about his experiences.

Full rhymes sound positive — they're making progress.

5   only then would he let me explore
the blown hinge of his lower jaw,

Repeated structure of two verbs in each stanza conveys the idea that she takes an active part in helping the soldier to get better.

and handle and hold
the damaged, porcelain collar-bone,

Images of the soldier's damaged body highlight how fragile he is. The fact that his body is broken down into a series of separate, broken objects suggests that war dehumanises people.

10   and mind and attend
the fractured rudder of shoulder-blade,

Personal pronoun shows the speaker is actively involved in her husband's recovery.

A damaged parachute would be useless.

and finger and thumb
the parachute silk of his punctured lung.

Figurative language suggests she's patching him up — it's as if she's tying his broken ribs back in place to make him strong again.

Comparing his ribs to the rungs of a ladder implies that his recovery is a slow, step-by-step process.

Only then could I bind the struts
and climb the rungs of his broken ribs,

Metaphor comparing the bullet to a foetus emphasises that his experiences are now a part of him. It could also hint that being injured is as life-changing as becoming a parent.

15   and feel the hurt
of his grazed heart.

Half-rhyme could reflect that she's partially understood the link between his physical and emotional pain, but there's still a way to go.

Skirting along,
only then could I picture the scan,

Image of a sweating bomb shows the tension and stress which his memories cause. He may not have dealt with some parts of his experience, as the mine is "unexploded".

20   the foetus of metal beneath his chest
where the bullet had finally come to rest.

Double meaning of "grazed" — the bullet only 'grazed past' his heart, but it left emotional 'grazes' behind.

Then I widened the search,
traced the scarring back to its source

Extended metaphor — the speaker has found the source of the "river" from stanza 2. She's moving closer to the cause of his suffering, but it also shows he's not better.

His emotional injuries are hidden — it's difficult to get to this part of him.

to a sweating, unexploded mine
buried deep in his mind, around which

25   every nerve in his body had tightened and closed.
Then, and only then, did I come close.

Enjambment across stanzas gives the poem a sense of movement, reflecting the speaker's desire to keep making progress, even if it's slow.

This is the only sentence that lies on one line. This gives emphasis to the wife's realisation that her husband's psychological 'scars' are worse than his physical ones.

The last lines don't fully rhyme, which makes this a muted ending — the speaker has made progress but can only "come close".

Context — Effects of War on Soldiers
Although it isn't set in any particular time, the poem addresses common issues about the effects of war on soldiers' bodies and minds. It was originally aired as part of a television documentary, read by Laura, the wife of soldier Eddie Beddoes, who was injured while serving in the army. He suffered from depression and post-traumatic stress disorder (PTSD) as a result of his experiences. PTSD is a condition triggered by stressful or frightening events, and it affects many soldiers.

POEM DICTIONARY
parachute silk — material used for parachutes before the invention of nylon
struts — rods or bars designed to resist pressure and help maintain a framework's structure

Section One — The Poems

Simon Armitage

Simon Armitage is an English poet, playwright and novelist. 'The Manhunt' is from his 2008 collection, *The Not Dead*, which looks at how war affects ex-soldiers, particularly those involved in recent conflicts.

You've got to know what the poem's about

1) The <u>wife of a soldier</u> gets to know her husband again after he returns home <u>injured</u> from war. The poem is sometimes subtitled 'Laura's Poem' — <u>Laura</u> (the soldier's wife) is the <u>speaker</u>.

2) Her husband has <u>physical</u> scars from the injuries he sustained in war.

3) He also has <u>psychological</u> 'scars' as a result of his <u>traumatic</u> experiences. The poem progresses from describing the scars on his <u>body</u> to exploring his <u>mental</u> 'scars' and how they <u>affect</u> him.

Learn about the form, structure and language

1) **FORM** — The poem's <u>couplet-long stanzas</u> have lines of <u>varying lengths</u>. Initially the couplets rhyme, but later on the rhymes <u>break down</u>, making the poem feel <u>disjointed</u> and reflecting the theme of <u>brokenness</u>. <u>Stanza breaks</u> between the couplets reflect the <u>distance</u> between the couple, but the <u>enjambment</u> indicates that there is <u>still a connection</u> between them.

2) **STRUCTURE** — Different <u>injuries</u> are introduced in different <u>couplets</u>, gradually moving <u>further</u> into the soldier's body. This allows the reader to <u>explore</u> his <u>body</u> and <u>mind</u> in the same slow process as his wife.

3) **LANGUAGE ABOUT THE BODY** — The soldier's body is presented using <u>adjectives</u> that describe <u>damage</u>. These are paired with <u>metaphors</u> that suggest his body has become a collection of <u>broken objects</u>. This could suggest that the damage has <u>taken away</u> some of his <u>humanity</u>, or these comparisons could be a way for his wife to <u>understand</u> and come to terms with his <u>injuries</u>.

4) **CARING LANGUAGE** — A range of different <u>verbs</u> are used to describe how the woman is <u>caring</u> for the injured man. Verbs like "trace" and "attend" are <u>gentle</u>, while "bind" shows how she is helping him to <u>regain his strength</u>. These words stress how <u>carefully</u> and <u>delicately</u> she cares for him.

Remember the feelings and attitudes in the poem

1) **LOVE** — The soldier's wife is <u>sensitive</u> in her approach to her wounded husband. She wants to <u>help</u> him and is slowly trying to get to <u>know</u> him again, in order to <u>understand</u> what he is going through.

2) **PATIENCE** — It takes the <u>whole poem</u> for the woman to just "<u>come close</u>" to her husband, and it's <u>unclear</u> how much more <u>progress</u> she will be able to make in the future. This shows how <u>patient</u> both the soldier and his wife will have to be for him to <u>recover</u> fully.

3) **PAIN** — The <u>imagery</u> in the poem suggests that the soldier suffers both <u>physically</u> and <u>mentally</u>. It's implied that his psychological trauma, rather than his physical pain, is the <u>main cause</u> of his suffering.

Go a step further and give a personal response

Have a go at <u>answering</u> these <u>questions</u> to help you come up with <u>your own ideas</u> about the poem:

Q1.   Why do you think the poet called this poem 'The Manhunt'?

Q2.   What impression does the reader get of the soldier's wife?

Q3.   Do you think the end of the poem is hopeful? Explain your answer.

Distance, suffering, romantic love...

'One Flesh' and 'A Complaint' also cover the theme of emotional suffering. The parent in 'Nettles' is still hurt by a memory of the past — compare this to how the soldier still suffers due to his memories of war.

My Father Would Not Show Us

Rainer Maria Rilke (1875-1926) was a poet and novelist who wrote philosophically about human existence. This quotation considers how to approach the dead and how to talk to / about them.

Alliteration makes the phrase sound heavy and lifeless, reflecting the subject matter.

Which way do we face to talk to the dead?
Rainer Maria Rilke

Passive — the situation isn't under narrator's control. Language is impersonal and hints at a lack of emotion.

Unsettling image — sounds sinister and makes the reader think of nightmares or horror films.

My father's face
five days dead
is organised for me to see.

The room is cold to preserve the body, but cold could also hint at the lifelessness or lack of emotion in the relationship.

Very matter-of-fact — focus on the details of the coffin rather than any kind of emotion.

5 It's cold in here
and the borrowed coffin gleams unnaturally;
the pine one has not yet been delivered.

Image of the father's dead, distorted face makes the death seem real and graphic.

Strong, definitive statement — the father's death marks a significant moment in the child's life.

Half-expected this inverted face
but not the soft, for some reason
unfrozen collar of his striped pyjamas.

Softness suggests intimacy — the narrator is close enough to see these details. Pyjamas also make the body seem more human.

The narrator perhaps sees the father's silence as fearful — could be seen as a criticism of the older, more private generation.

10 This is the last time I am allowed
to remember my childhood as it might have been:
a louder, braver place,
crowded, a house with a tin roof
being hailed upon, and voices rising,
15 my father's wry smile, his half-turned face.

Suggests that the narrator's childhood was not a happy one. Imagining how it "might have been" implies that it was the opposite of these things — a quiet, empty house.

Repetition suggests disappointment or disbelief — the narrator finds it difficult to understand the father's behaviour.

My father would not show us how to die.
He hid, he hid away.
Behind the curtains where his life had been,
the florist's flowers curling into spring,
20 he lay inside, he lay.

Father's attention is elsewhere, not where the narrator wants it to be — reflects child's desire to be the focus of a parent's attention.

Suggests that there were certain things he 'could' do, but helping his children to understand and prepare for his death was not one of them.

He could recall the rag-and-bone man
passing his mother's gate in the morning light.
Now the tunnelling sound of the dogs next door;
everything he hears is white.

Ambiguous title is expanded on. Collective disappointment of the children ("us") that their father wouldn't guide them as a parent normally would.

Synesthesia (the linking of two or more senses for effect) is used in this line as the father hears colour — perhaps to show the blurring of the senses as he dies.

25 My father could not show us how to die.
He turned, he turned away.
Under the counterpane, without one call
or word or name,
face to the wall, he lay.

Language of death — "tunnelling" hints at burial and "white" suggests blankness but is also associated with heaven.

Repeats line 16, but use of "could not" instead of "would not" suggests that the narrator's opinion is softening, or perhaps they are beginning to understand his reasons.

The change from "would not" to "could not" makes the reader reconsider the father's behaviour — perhaps he "turned away" to protect his children from the pain of watching him die.

Subdued closing phrase reflects the subdued ending to his life. This also echoes line 20, emphasising that his behaviour did not change.

Even as he was dying, he didn't speak any last words or call out for his family.

POEM DICTIONARY
wry — sarcastic, amused or mocking
rag-and-bone man — in the past, a person who travelled around buying old or unwanted clothes and household goods
counterpane — bedspread

Ingrid de Kok

Ingrid de Kok is a South African poet who writes a mixture of political and personal poetry. She's also a professor at the University of Cape Town. 'My Father Would Not Show Us' was first published in 1988.

You've got to know what the poem's about

1) The poem describes the narrator's experience seeing their father's dead <u>body</u>.

2) The narrator reflects on their <u>childhood</u> and hints that their <u>relationship</u> with their father was <u>not perfect</u>.

3) They try to <u>understand</u> their father's <u>behaviour</u> and inability to connect with his children as he was <u>dying</u>.

Learn about the form, structure and language

1) **FORM** — The poem is written in <u>free verse</u> — it has <u>no regular</u> stanza length or rhyme scheme. This <u>lack of order</u> reflects the <u>disruption</u> that death causes and alludes to the <u>complexity</u> of the <u>emotions</u> involved — they <u>cannot be organised</u> simply and neatly. The use of a <u>first-person</u> voice gives a strong sense of the narrator's <u>personal</u> thoughts and experiences.

2) **STRUCTURE** — The poem moves from the <u>present</u> situation to past <u>memories</u>, some of which may be <u>imagined</u> (e.g. in stanza 4). There is a sense of <u>frustration</u> throughout, but there are <u>hints</u> that the narrator reaches a new, more <u>sympathetic understanding</u> towards the end (line 25).

3) **REPETITION** — Repetition is used in the poem to highlight the narrator's <u>frustration</u> with their <u>father</u> as he "hid" and "turned away". The poem's <u>title</u> is also repeated in lines 16 and 25, but the exact wording <u>changes</u> — this perhaps demonstrates the narrator's <u>growing understanding</u> of their father's behaviour.

4) **LANGUAGE OF THE SENSES** — The narrator uses <u>sensory language</u> throughout the poem to create vivid <u>imagery</u>. It helps the reader <u>imagine</u> the situation and therefore <u>empathise</u> with the narrator. It also brings the narrator's <u>imagined memories</u> to life, suggesting they have thought deeply about them.

Remember the feelings and attitudes in the poem

1) **GRIEF** — Despite the <u>emotional distance</u> between them when he was alive, the narrator <u>feels the loss</u> of their father keenly. They <u>grieve</u> for their father, but also for how their relationship <u>could have been</u>.

2) **FRUSTRATION** — The father's <u>desire for privacy</u> is <u>hard</u> for his children to <u>accept</u> as they were so <u>detached</u> from his death. There may also be frustration that <u>older generations</u> can be more <u>private</u> about <u>personal matters</u>, which younger generations often struggle to understand.

3) **UNDERSTANDING** — The <u>change</u> from "<u>would not</u> show us" to "<u>could not</u> show us" suggests that the father <u>did not know how</u> to share his experiences with his children, and hints that the <u>narrator</u> is reaching a <u>sense of understanding</u>. This heightens the sense of <u>sadness</u> as they are only just <u>starting to understand</u> him now that he is <u>dead</u>.

Go a step further and give a personal response

Have a go at <u>answering</u> these <u>questions</u> to help you come up with <u>your own ideas</u> about the poem:

Q1.	To what extent do you think the narrator wishes that their father had acted differently?
Q2.	Why do you think the poet has included a quotation at the start?
Q3.	How does the narrator uses language to show uncertainty in the poem?

Family relationships, death and suffering, memory...

Take a look at 'A Child to his Sick Grandfather' and consider how the two narrators react to the death of a loved one. You could also compare the narrator's sadness with the reaction to loss in 'A Complaint'.

Practice Questions

Phew, that's all the poems covered... Take a breath and get cracking on these next few pages — there are a few questions on each of the poems. Make sure you're happy with them all before you move on.

La Belle Dame Sans Merci

1) Give a brief summary of what the poem is about.

2) What is the effect of having different voices speaking in the poem?

3) How does the poem show the knight's sense of despair after his experience? Give two examples.

A Child to his Sick Grandfather

1) Briefly explain what happens in the poem.

2) What do the child's questions indicate about their relationship with their grandfather?

3) What effect does the repetition of "dad" have in the poem?

She Walks in Beauty

1) What do you think the poem's overall message is?

2) The poem uses both dark and light imagery to describe the woman. What effect does this have?

3) Find an example of a sound device in the poem and explain its effect.

A Complaint

1) What "change" is the narrator referring to in the poem?

2) Find an example of direct address in the poem and explain its effect.

3) What effect does the rhyme scheme of the poem have?

Neutral Tones

1) What do you think Hardy is saying about the nature of love?

2) How does the narrator convey a sense of lifelessness and pessimism?

3) What does it mean to say the poem's structure is 'cyclical'? What is the effect of this structure?

Practice Questions

Sonnet 43

1) Give a summary of what the narrator says in the poem.

2) Do you think the narrator expects something in return from their lover? Explain your answer.

3) How does Barrett Browning use hyperbole in the poem?

My Last Duchess

1) What do you think happened to the Duke's last Duchess? Give evidence to support your answer.

2) Describe what we learn about the Duchess's character. Is this likely to be a fair view?

3) What is the effect of the poem being written in rhyming couplets?

First Date – She / First Date – He

1) Briefly explain what the poems are about.

2) Describe how the speakers show their lack of confidence in the poems.

3) Find three examples of repetition between the poems and explain the effect they have.

Valentine

1) Give a short explanation of the extended metaphor that is used in the poem.

2) How does the mood change throughout the poem?

3) Using examples from the poem, explain how the narrator views traditional romantic gifts.

One Flesh

1) Briefly describe the situation that the narrator presents in the poem.

2) Find an example of a simile in the poem and explain its effect.

3) What effect does religious language have on the overall tone of the poem?

Practice Questions

i wanna be yours

1) Briefly explain the speaker's main message in the poem.

2) Find an example of an image that surprises you in the poem and explain why.

3) What is the effect of the use of slang in the poem?

Love's Dog

1) How does the poet present a realistic idea of love in the poem?

2) Pick two images from the poem and explain their possible meanings.

3) How does the irregularity of the rhyme scheme support the poem's message?

Nettles

1) Describe the extended metaphor in the poem and explain the effect it has on the reader.

2) Using examples, describe how sound devices are used in the poem to support its meaning.

3) How is the parent's love for their son conveyed in the poem? Find examples to justify your answer.

The Manhunt

1) How does the poet convey the fragility of the solider?

2) What is the effect of the repetition in stanzas 4-6?

3) What does the enjambment between stanzas suggest about the couple's relationship?

My Father Would Not Show Us

1) Briefly describe the mood of the poem.

2) Explain the difference between "would not" (line 16) and "could not" (line 25). What is the effect of this change on the reader?

3) What is the effect of describing the flowers as "curling into spring" (line 19)?

Practice Questions

Here's a page of exam-style questions for you now. You don't have to do these all at once — just do them in a way that suits you. Before you start, here are some important things you need to remember:

In each of your answers, you should write about how poets use language, structure and form, and the effects these create for the reader. It's also important to include some ideas about context — think about how the poets might have been influenced by things like history, culture and their own experiences.

Exam-style Questions

1) Compare how negative emotions are portrayed in 'Valentine' and one other poem from 'Relationships'.

2) Explore the ways in which the difficulties of love are portrayed in 'La Belle Dame Sans Merci' and one other poem from 'Relationships'.

3) Compare the portrayal of a relationship that changes over time in 'A Complaint' and one other poem from 'Relationships'.

4) Discuss the ways a fragile relationship is presented in 'The Manhunt' compared to one other poem from 'Relationships'.

5) Compare how family relationships are portrayed in 'My Father Would Not Show Us' and one other poem from 'Relationships'.

Romantic Love

If, like me, you're bitter and don't only want to read about happy, smug people in love, then you're in luck...

1) <u>A lot</u> of poetry is written about romantic love — not surprising as it's one of the most <u>intense</u> feelings we can have.

2) People have <u>different experiences</u> of romantic love.

Anyone else think 'romance' sounds like 'no thanks'?

Romantic love can have an element of danger

Valentine (Pages 18-19)

1) The narrator paints a <u>realistic picture</u> of love, acknowledging that alongside the "light" it promises, sometimes it can "<u>blind you with tears</u>". This image suggests that romantic love can be <u>upsetting</u> or <u>harmful</u>.

2) The onion's "<u>fierce kiss</u>" has <u>threatening</u> connotations. This personification hints at the <u>potential dangers</u> of passion, emphasising that love has the power to cause <u>pain</u>.

3) The poem ends with the <u>sinister image</u> of the <u>knife</u> and the idea that love can be "Lethal". This closes the poem on an <u>unsettling</u> note as it implies that <u>physical violence</u> and <u>threat</u> is part of the relationship.

My Last Duchess (Pages 14-15)

1) The Duke's romantic <u>relationship</u> with the Duchess became <u>destructive</u> after his desire turned into <u>jealousy</u>. The former Duchess's fate isn't <u>fully explained</u>, but the Duke's <u>anger</u> and <u>sinister</u> phrases, e.g. "<u>Then all smiles stopped together</u>", strongly indicate that he has had her <u>killed</u>.

2) The poem's <u>form</u> emphasises the Duke's sinister nature. <u>Strict couplets</u> indicate his need for <u>control</u>, but <u>enjambment disrupts</u> them, hinting that he may be dangerously <u>unstable</u>.

3) After his wife's death, the Duke has <u>full control</u> over her. He controls everything her portrait 'sees', which contrasts with his <u>lack of control</u> over where she "<u>looked</u>" when she was alive.

It isn't always clear if love is romantic or not

A Complaint (Pages 8-9)

1) <u>Many critics believe</u> that the poem is written about a <u>friend</u> rather than a lover (see p.9), but this isn't explicitly stated in the poem, and it could be read with a <u>romantic interpretation</u>.

2) The narrator remembers the "<u>murmuring, sparkling, living</u> love" they shared with the other person with fondness. These <u>lively</u> but <u>gentle</u> adjectives indicate the narrator's passion and tenderness.

3) The use of <u>romantic language</u> to describe a <u>friendship</u> could emphasise how <u>important</u> it was to the narrator — they perhaps feel the <u>loss</u> of it as <u>strongly</u> as if it had been a romantic relationship.

She Walks in Beauty (Pages 6-7)

1) The narrator enthusiastically describes the woman's <u>physical beauty</u> and "<u>nameless grace</u>", which hints at his <u>romantic feelings</u> towards her.

2) The woman is described as "<u>pure</u>", and the narrator refers to her "<u>mind</u>" and "<u>heart</u>" — the narrator shows an <u>awareness</u> of her perfect <u>personality</u> as well as her physical <u>appearance</u>.

3) However, the narrator's actual <u>feelings</u> towards her are <u>unstated</u> — whilst he evidently admires her personality and physical beauty, the strength of his <u>romantic feelings</u> towards her is unclear.

Romantic Love

Romantic love isn't always straightforward

Love's Dog (Pages 24-25)

1) The narrator talks about what they "love" and what they "hate" about love, making it clear that the two are closely linked by discussing them both within the same couplets.

2) The imagery in the poem is complex and unconventional — the reader must work out what each image symbolises about love, as it isn't immediately clear. This suggests that love is too complicated to be easily categorised or described.

The Manhunt (Pages 28-29)

1) The poem explores the complicated relationship between a married couple who are reconnecting after the husband has returned from war — the soldier has been changed by his experiences.

2) The reference to "passionate nights and intimate days" suggests that the physical side of their relationship was not negatively affected by the husband's experiences. However, the image of the "grazed heart" suggests that their emotional connection took longer to recover.

3) The narrator works through her husband's physical injuries before following his emotional scarring "back to its source". This is a slow and difficult process which highlights that love can require patience and dedication.

Sonnet 43 (Pages 12-13)

1) At times, the speaker seems to struggle to explain her love. The question at the start of the poem ("How do I love thee?") indicates that she is trying to work out how to express her feelings, before deciding that a list is the easiest method to "count the ways".

2) Caesurae in the final lines break up the flow of the poem, suggesting that the speaker is struggling to articulate her feelings — she is so excited by her love that it affects her ability to communicate.

Clichéd imagery isn't for everyone

Valentine (Pages 18-19)

1) The speaker challenges the stereotypical ideas of romantic love by offering their lover "an onion". The offer of such an ordinary, domestic object, rather than "a red rose or a satin heart", suggests that they are trying to find a more original and authentic way to show their love.

2) The speaker claims they are "trying to be truthful" — this suggests that they believe that traditional romantic gifts such as a "cute card or a kissogram" are untruthful.

i wanna be yours (Pages 22-23)

1) The narrator seems to deliberately avoid using clichés or traditional imagery to express their feelings. Instead, they use everyday objects, e.g. a "coffee pot" and a "raincoat", to explain their love.

2) They list ways they want to be useful to their lover, highlighting their devotion, but also emphasising that they believe their everyday presence is more valuable than extravagant gestures.

Other poems also feature love in various forms...

Family relationships can feature similar feelings to romantic ones. 'Nettles' shows a parent caring for and trying to protect their son, while 'My Father Would Not Show Us' is about a difficult relationship.

Family Relationships

On to a different sort of love, but still lots of emotions flying around. No creepy murderers though. Phew.

1) There's sometimes <u>tension</u> in family relationships, but there's also <u>closeness</u> and <u>love</u>.
2) Relationships between <u>family members</u> can <u>change</u> over time.

Parents try to protect their children in different ways

Nettles (Pages 26-27)

1) The parent's <u>violent destruction</u> of the nettles is a <u>powerful</u> and <u>protective</u> reaction to the child's "sobs and tears". Emotive phrases such as "<u>slashed in fury</u>" show how they destroyed the <u>enemy</u> that harmed their child in an attempt to <u>protect</u> him from <u>further pain</u>.

2) However, the poem <u>ends</u> with the parent reflecting that they <u>couldn't protect</u> their son from all "sharp wounds" — they were perhaps only able to offer "<u>comfort</u>" rather than protection.

My Father Would Not Show Us (Pages 30-31)

1) Despite the seeming lack of <u>emotional connection</u> between the father and his children, his <u>actions</u> ("He hid, he hid away") could be an attempt to <u>shield</u> them from the pain of watching him die.

2) The phrase "<u>would not</u>" shows a deliberate <u>act of will</u>. This <u>contrasts</u> with the <u>helplessness</u> and lack of control in dying — one thing he can try to <u>control</u> is the amount of <u>pain</u> his children suffer.

3) The narrator seems to resent their father's "face to the wall" approach, but reaches a better <u>understanding</u> about him in the final stanza, when they say that he "<u>could not</u>" show them. This suggests that they begin to take a more <u>sympathetic</u> viewpoint — perhaps seeing his <u>silence</u> as <u>helpless</u> and his <u>hiding</u> as an attempt to <u>protect</u> his children.

It can be difficult to watch family members grow old

One Flesh (Pages 20-21)

1) The narrator explores how their parents' <u>relationship</u> has <u>changed</u> with age — the couple are "<u>cool</u>" and "<u>hardly ever touch</u>", which <u>contrasts</u> strongly with their "<u>fire</u>" and "<u>former passion</u>".

2) There is <u>sadness</u> in the narrator's tone when they discuss that the "<u>Chastity</u>" between the couple has been an inevitable "<u>destination</u>".

3) At the end of the poem, the narrator is <u>reflective</u> as they wonder if their parents "<u>know they're old</u>" — the narrator seems <u>more aware</u> of this fact than their parents are themselves.

A Child to his Sick Grandfather (Pages 4-5)

1) The speaker remembers the <u>happy</u>, <u>loving</u> relationship they had with their grandfather during their <u>childhood</u> — they recall how he "<u>used to smile</u>" and affectionately "<u>stroke</u>" their head.

2) The speaker is "<u>vexed</u>" by the sight of their grandfather now he is <u>elderly</u>, which indicates their <u>distress</u> and <u>frustration</u> at the situation. It is <u>painful</u> for them to watch him <u>struggle</u>.

Other poems also involve an element of protection...

'The Manhunt' is about a husband and wife, but also shows an attempt to care for and protect someone. In 'i wanna be yours', the speaker uses metaphors to do with care and protection to express their love.

Section Two — Themes

Memory

You may look back fondly on your time spent studying poetry, or it may haunt you for the rest of your days.

> 1) Memories can appear in <u>different ways</u> and can be hard to <u>forget</u>.
>
> 2) <u>Strong emotions</u> can be caused by people's memories.

Painful memories show themselves in different ways

Neutral Tones (Pages 10-11)

1) The narrator vividly remembers the <u>end</u> of their relationship and the <u>setting</u> in which it happened — they describe the <u>expression</u> on their lover's face and the <u>pond</u> "edged with grayish leaves".

2) This <u>memory returns</u> to them whenever love goes "<u>wrong</u>" — for them, it is a <u>symbol</u> of <u>failed love</u>.

3) The memory is <u>bitter</u> and <u>pessimistic</u>. Even the <u>sun</u>, a symbol of warmth and light, is "<u>God-curst</u>" — this hints that the narrator feels their <u>life</u> has been <u>cursed</u> by the memory of the break-up.

The Manhunt (Pages 28-29)

1) The <u>physical scars</u> on the soldier's "damaged" and "fractured" body are <u>visual reminders</u> of war, hinting at memories of <u>violence</u> and <u>destruction</u>.

2) The soldier's <u>psychological scars</u> are also significant — his memories are "<u>buried deep in his mind</u>", which suggests that they are <u>difficult</u> to deal with and move on from.

3) The powerful image of the "<u>sweating, unexploded mine</u>" shows how <u>deeply</u> his memories affect him — the mine is "unexploded", which suggests that it has the <u>potential</u> to cause <u>more harm</u> in the future.

Memories can stir up difficult emotions

My Father Would Not Show Us (Pages 30-31)

> 1) The poem explores the narrator's <u>memories</u> of their father, such as how he "hid away" from his children. This is mentioned repeatedly, highlighting how <u>upset</u> they were by his behaviour.
>
> 2) In the fourth stanza, the narrator describes <u>imagined</u> and <u>idealised</u> memories, choosing to remember their childhood as it "<u>might have been</u>" rather than as it was. It is perhaps a <u>comfort</u> to imagine the past differently, e.g. as a "louder, braver place".
>
> 3) In the penultimate stanza, the narrator imagines their <u>father's memories</u> of the "rag-and-bone man", which could show how his <u>focus</u> is in the <u>past</u>, rather than the present where his children need him.

Nettles (Pages 26-27)

> 1) The narrator recalls events of the past <u>chronologically</u> and <u>clearly</u>, describing details such as the child's age and his "watery grin". <u>Memories</u> usually become <u>unclear</u> over time, so this <u>detailed recollection</u> could show the <u>depth</u> of their <u>frustration</u> that their son was hurt.
>
> 2) The narrator <u>recalls</u> their "<u>fury</u>" clearly, emphasising how <u>strong</u> their emotions were at the time.
>
> 3) The whole poem is a <u>memory</u>, but the final line highlights that it is not an <u>isolated</u> one — it could be <u>replaced</u> by other anecdotes about times when the parents have been distressed by their child's pain.

Think about the theme of memory in other poems...

The narrators of 'A Complaint' and 'A Child to his Sick Grandfather' both describe happy memories with someone they love, before showing how different things have become in each relationship.

Desire and Longing

I'm consumed by desire and longing... the crunchy base... the creamy filling... ohhh sweet cheesecake.

> 1) Desire is often <u>positive</u> and can show how <u>deeply</u> people <u>care</u> about each other.
>
> 2) However, desire and longing can sometimes have <u>terrible effects</u>.

Desire and longing can show the depth of someone's love...

i wanna be yours (Pages 22-23)

1) The <u>repetition</u> of phrases like "<u>let me be your</u>" and "<u>i wanna be yours</u>" shows the speaker's <u>urgent longing</u> to belong to the other person. It sounds as though the speaker is <u>pleading</u> with them, <u>desperate</u> for a positive response.

2) The speaker repeats the word "<u>deep</u>" in the final stanza, emphasising the <u>strength</u> of their <u>emotions</u>.

3) The <u>final stanza</u> is also <u>longer</u> than the others, emphasising the speaker's <u>enthusiastic</u> desire — as the speaker gets <u>caught up</u> in their "deep devotion", they become more <u>passionate</u> and <u>agitated</u>.

A Child to his Sick Grandfather (Pages 4-5)

1) The narrator <u>longs</u> for their grandfather to "<u>Rouse up</u>" and <u>get better</u>, which indicates the <u>depth</u> of their <u>love</u> for him.

2) The <u>pleading tone</u> in the question "<u>You will not die and leave us then?</u>" shows how much the child wants the grandfather to recover — they can't bear the thought of being without him.

3) The narrator's <u>positive descriptions</u> of spending time with their grandfather are <u>pleasant</u>, e.g. how he used to "smile" and "stroke" their head. This may explain why the narrator <u>longs</u> for his <u>recovery</u>.

...but they can be destructive

My Last Duchess (Pages 14-15)

1) The Duke longed for <u>control</u> over his wife and her total <u>obedience</u>. A level of <u>physical desire</u> for the Duchess is also indicated by his references to parts of her <u>body</u>, e.g. her "cheek" and "throat".

2) Desire is also what <u>destroyed</u> his trust in their <u>relationship</u> as he became <u>jealous</u>, suspecting that "she liked whate'er / She looked on". His desire not to <u>share</u> her and to retain <u>ownership</u> over her, both <u>physically</u> and <u>mentally</u>, may have driven him to have her <u>killed</u>.

La Belle Dame Sans Merci (Pages 2-3)

1) The knight in the poem <u>longs</u> for the "beautiful" lady but is left "<u>haggard</u>" and "<u>woe-begone</u>" after she <u>abandons</u> him.

2) The <u>consequences</u> of his desire have affected him <u>physically</u> — Keats uses the images of a "lily" and a "fading rose" to illustrate how <u>pale</u> and <u>unwell</u> he looks.

3) The knight's longing gives the lady <u>power</u> over him — he is said to be "<u>in thrall</u>" to her. His desire means he <u>ignores warnings</u> about her and ultimately leads to his <u>destruction</u>.

Feelings of desire and longing are present in other poems...

In 'Sonnet 43', the speaker's description of her love suggests powerful longing. In 'First Date – She / First Date – He', the couple seem to desire to be together, but don't realise they both feel the same way.

Adoration

I just adore writing about other people's love. Alright, fine, I don't — but just like you, I've got to do it...

> 1) Some people are completely <u>adoring</u> of those they <u>love</u>.
> 2) Sometimes, adoration is felt so <u>intensely</u> that it almost becomes <u>worship</u>.

Adoration can be a part of a romantic relationship

Sonnet 43 (Pages 12-13)

1) The <u>repetition</u> of "<u>I love thee</u>" at the beginnings of lines (anaphora) is a key feature of the poem — it emphasises the <u>depth</u> of the speaker's <u>adoration</u> of her lover.

2) The speaker is <u>enthusiastic</u> in her "<u>passion</u>" — her devotion is so strong that she will love him even "<u>better after death</u>".

3) She loves him even on an <u>ordinary</u>, <u>domestic</u> level ("to the level of everyday's / Most quiet need"). This shows how her <u>whole life</u> is <u>dedicated</u> to him.

Sonnet 44 — "I love thee more than doughnuts..."

i wanna be yours (Pages 22-23)

1) The image of the speaker "<u>breathing in</u>" someone's "<u>dust</u>" is <u>intimate</u> — it hints at how <u>close</u> the speaker wants to be to the person in the poem.

2) The image of the "<u>teddy bear</u>" that goes "<u>anywhere</u>" with the person suggests that the speaker wants to spend all their <u>time</u> with them, indicating the <u>depth</u> of their adoration.

Adoration can look like religious worship

She Walks in Beauty (Pages 6-7)

1) The speaker suggests that the woman is <u>divine</u>. He describes the way that her mind is "at peace with <u>all below</u>", which could imply she's <u>above</u> everyone else, possibly like an angel or goddess.

2) The use of <u>hyperbole</u> in "all that's <u>best</u> of dark and bright" shows that the woman described is <u>perfect</u>. The speaker focuses on <u>different parts</u> of the <u>woman's body</u>, such as her "raven tress" and her "cheek" — each one is <u>worthy</u> of being <u>worshipped</u>.

A Complaint (Pages 8-9)

1) When the speaker describes their <u>love</u> as a "<u>consecrated fount</u>" (a sacred fountain), they imply that it is <u>divine</u> and therefore <u>worthy of worship</u>. It could also be a reference to <u>holy water</u>, suggesting that the water is sacred and <u>purifies</u> those that it touches.

2) The speaker thinks they were "<u>Blest</u>" to have felt the love they had with the other person. This language equates the blessing of their love to a <u>gift received from God</u>. The phrase "<u>bliss above</u>" could also refer to <u>heaven</u>, again <u>elevating</u> the speaker's feelings to a <u>sacred</u> level.

OTHER POEMS

Adoration is also shown in 'La Belle Dame Sans Merci'...

The knight in 'La Belle Dame Sans Merci' completely adores the lady he meets. However, his adoration is so strong that he misses the warning signs about her, leading to his despair when she abandons him.

Death and Suffering

It's not all roses in these poems, there's actually quite a lot of death and suffering going around...

> 1) People react differently to death and can find it hard to understand.
>
> 2) Suffering can be physical, emotional or both — and it's not always just the person directly affected who suffers.

Death can be difficult to understand

A Child to his Sick Grandfather (Pages 4-5)

1) The child is aware of the grandfather's ill health and shows sadness over how "frail" he is — they are "vexed" to see him in his current state.

2) They can't understand why their grandfather's behaviour has changed ("I wot not how it be") — this shows that they perhaps can't grasp how suffering affects people.

3) They try to plead with their grandfather in the hope that they can change his mind and he won't "leave". This suggests that the narrator is too young to fully understand death.

My Father Would Not Show Us (Pages 30-31)

1) The narrator has not been involved in their father's suffering or death ("He hid, he hid away"), and so finds it hard to understand. As a result, there are some aspects of his death that they "Half-expected", but others are surprising, e.g. the "unfrozen collar" of the father's pyjamas.

2) Near the end of the poem, the narrator begins to recognise that the father "could not" share the experience of dying with them — perhaps because he did not understand it himself.

3) The way the father suffers in silence ("without one call") may reflect the way older generations tend to be more private about personal matters. This may be hard for the younger narrator to understand.

Death imagery can emphasise suffering or danger

Neutral Tones (Pages 10-11)

1) Hardy uses language to do with death to show the loss of love between the narrator and their lover. The narrator describes their lover's "smile" as "the deadest thing / Alive" — this oxymoron emphasises the lover's complete lack of feeling for the narrator.

2) The lifeless and decaying winter landscape reflects the death of their love — the leaves are "gray" and even the sun is cold and "white", offering no warmth or vitality. The "starving sod" lacks the nourishment needed for life — this hints that their relationship didn't have enough love to keep it alive.

Valentine (Pages 18-19)

1) The description of the onion as "Lethal" emphasises the element of danger that can be involved in a relationship, such as that it can be overly "possessive" or take over someone's life.

2) The poem also uses the image of a "knife", which has connotations of pain and death. This is shocking in a love poem and could show how real, honest love ("I am trying to be truthful") has the potential to be destructive.

3) The image of the knife could also emphasise that people in love are vulnerable, as they would be when faced with a knife.

Death and Suffering

Love can cause people to suffer

La Belle Dame Sans Merci (Pages 2-3)

1) The knight's "anguish" is clear from the start of the poem — he is described as "haggard" and "woe-begone" by the narrator.

2) The poem is structured as an answer to a question ("what can ail thee, knight-at-arms?"). The knight reveals his story over the course of the poem, which explains that his suffering is rooted in his experiences with the lady.

3) The image of the "fading rose" highlights his loss — a rose is a symbol of love and romance, but here it fades, which subverts these joyful images and shows that heartache has taken their place.

As if having to dress in this get-up wasn't suffering enough...

Love's Dog (Pages 24-25)

1) The poem begins and ends with images of sickness — the speaker perhaps views love as an illness.

2) The speaker uses medical language such as "diagnosis" and "prognosis" to describe the experience of love. The speaker seems to link love to an incurable disease, hinting that they suffer physically and emotionally because of it.

3) The image of the "sick parrot" could suggest that the speaker is lovesick and that they may resent the feeling — they don't like the sense of being overwhelmed by love.

It's painful to watch someone you love suffer

Nettles (Pages 26-27)

1) The poem describes how the parents "soothed" their son after he was hurt. The phrase "At last" implies how relieved they are to see their son "grin" again and indicates that it was difficult for them to watch him suffer.

2) The narrator's frenzied destruction of the nettles in reaction to their child's pain ("slashed in fury") shows how deeply they care for him and how his wellbeing affects their own. They channel their anguish at the child's suffering into anger.

The Manhunt (Pages 28-29)

1) The repetition of "only then" throughout the poem highlights the slow steps the wife must take to support her husband. The process of regaining their emotional closeness is made to sound laborious and difficult, showing how she is also suffering from her husband's injuries.

2) The detailed descriptions of his injuries (e.g. "blown hinge of his lower jaw") emphasise the extent of the damage to his body and show how difficult the task of supporting him through them must be.

3) She cares deeply for him, even feeling his pain as if it's her own — she says she could "feel the hurt" of his heart.

OTHER POEMS

Other poems also cover death or suffering...

'My Last Duchess' is framed around the story of the Duchess's death, which is used to explore the Duke's need for power. The couple in 'One Flesh' have also suffered a great loss of "passion" and closeness.

Distance and Separation

Sometimes I wish for some distance between me and these poems, but you just can't tear us apart.

> 1) People in relationships are sometimes <u>closer</u> than they initially <u>seem</u>.
> 2) <u>Distance</u> in relationships can't always be <u>overcome</u>.

Distance can seem bigger than it is...

One Flesh (Pages 20-21)

1) The couple's <u>passion</u> has "<u>grown cold</u>" — they are "Lying apart", which indicates both a <u>physical</u> and an <u>emotional distance</u> between them. The <u>caesura</u> which breaks the first line makes this distance more pronounced.

2) They "<u>hardly ever touch</u>", but they might not be completely separated. The simile comparing the <u>silence</u> between them to a "<u>thread</u>" they both "<u>hold</u>" suggests they are still connected <u>emotionally</u>.

First Date – She / First Date – He (Pages 16-17)

1) The speakers in the poems seem to be <u>emotionally distant</u> from one another, as each believes that the other is <u>not interested</u> in them, e.g. they each think the other is "<u>quite undistracted</u>" by them.

2) However, it is clear to the reader that the couple are <u>misinterpreting</u> the situation — while each speaker thinks the other is disinterested, the <u>opposite poem</u> reveals that they are <u>mistaken</u>. Close <u>repetition</u> between the poems emphasises how the couple are thinking and feeling <u>the same way</u>.

...but sometimes separation is permanent

La Belle Dame Sans Merci (Pages 2-3)

1) Following his <u>separation</u> from the lady, the knight's situation seems <u>hopeless</u> and <u>final</u>. <u>Nightmarish imagery</u> of previous victims' "starved lips in the gloom" and <u>bleak</u> surroundings where "no birds sing" are <u>ominous</u> and hint at his <u>despair</u>.

2) The <u>kings</u>, <u>princes</u> and <u>warriors</u> who appear to him in the dream seem <u>trapped</u> and alone. The knight has also found himself in the lady's "<u>thrall</u>", indicating that he is <u>condemned</u> to the same <u>isolation</u>.

3) The poem's <u>cyclical structure</u> reinforces the idea that he is <u>doomed</u> to be separated from the lady forever — his story is <u>framed</u> by desolate descriptions of his surroundings which give the impression that he <u>cannot escape</u>.

A Complaint (Pages 8-9)

1) The speaker has been <u>separated</u> from someone. The blunt statement "<u>There is a change</u>" shows the speaker's <u>certainty</u> that the love between the pair isn't as <u>lively</u> and <u>abundant</u> as it used to be.

2) The <u>caesura</u> in the first line of the poem hints at the <u>permanency</u> of the situation — the <u>long dash</u> after the first statement makes it seem final, emphasising the perpetual nature of the <u>separation</u>.

3) Even though the speaker's "well of love" for the person is "never dry", they <u>question</u> how <u>important</u> this is ("<u>What matter?</u>"). This indicates that any hope of <u>reconciliation</u> is slim and the <u>separation</u> is <u>likely</u> to be <u>permanent</u>.

Think about distance and separation in other poems...

The speaker in 'She Walks in Beauty' only admires the woman from a distance — their feelings may change when they get to know her. The couple in 'Neutral Tones' are also emotionally separated.

Negative Emotions

You might have some negative emotions towards poetry by now, but chin up — this section's almost done.

> 1) <u>Bitterness</u> can develop as the result of someone's <u>experiences</u> in a relationship.
>
> 2) People often experience <u>fear</u> if something happens that's out of their <u>control</u>.

Some people feel bitterness or hatred towards relationships

Love's Dog (Pages 24-25)

1) <u>Hate</u> is a <u>prominent</u> theme in the poem. It appears in <u>almost every couplet</u>, and the narrator lists a total of <u>seven</u> things they "hate" about love.

2) In one couplet, "<u>loathe</u>" replaces "hate" to create a more <u>passionate</u> and <u>emphatic</u> statement. The <u>alliteration</u> of "burnt toast and bonemeal" in this couplet sounds <u>bitter</u> — the <u>plosive</u> 'b' sounds are <u>harsh</u> and indicate the narrator's <u>resentment</u> towards these two domestic images. This could show their overall resentment of the <u>mundane</u>, <u>everyday</u> reality of relationships.

Neutral Tones (Pages 10-11)

1) The narrator's <u>bitterness</u> over the breakdown of their relationship is shown through the <u>pessimistic</u> tone of the poem. Their firm announcement that "<u>love deceives</u>" reflects their <u>ongoing hostility</u> towards love.

2) Descriptions of <u>nature</u> further emphasise the narrator's <u>bitterness</u> — the <u>sun</u>, normally a bright and joyful sight, is "<u>God-curst</u>" to them. Nature has lost its vibrancy and colour, offering instead <u>bleak</u>, "<u>gray</u>" leaves.

Rob and Joe had found one way to deal with their bitterness...

Love can make people fearful

First Date – She / First Date – He (Pages 16-17)

1) Both narrators suffer from a <u>lack of confidence</u> which makes them <u>fearful</u>. He fears that she is <u>more attractive</u> than him ("Perhaps she is out of my league"). She concentrates on the concert so that she'll "have something <u>clever</u> to say", which could imply her fear that she is <u>less intelligent</u> than he is.

2) She is <u>self-conscious</u> about the "<u>impression</u>" she gives off and he worries about how he might "<u>appear</u>" to her. They are both very <u>aware</u> of what the other person might be thinking and how they are being <u>perceived</u>, which makes them seem even more <u>nervous</u>.

One Flesh (Pages 20-21)

1) The <u>couple</u> in the poem seem <u>fearful</u> of their own relationship. They "<u>hardly ever touch</u>", which implies that they are <u>afraid</u> to show <u>affection</u> to each other. When they do touch, it is compared to a "<u>confession</u>", which indicates that they believe they are doing something <u>wrong</u>.

2) "<u>Chastity</u>" is presented as something to be feared — it "<u>faces them</u>" ominously and seems <u>inevitable</u>.

3) The <u>narrator</u> is the <u>couple's child</u>, so it could be argued that it is the child who is <u>fearful</u> — perhaps of the way that life seems to be "<u>a preparation</u>" for this stage of having <u>no passion</u> and <u>little hope</u>.

Other poems also include negative emotions...

The knight in 'La Belle Dame Sans Merci' is betrayed, which transforms his joy into despair. 'Valentine' introduces the idea of danger in relationships, which may reflect the negative emotions that can develop.

Practice Questions

It's the end of another section, so you know what that means — handy questions to see how well you've absorbed everything you've just read. Try to answer them without looking back through the section.

Romantic Love

1) What is the effect of Duffy's use of sinister imagery in 'Valentine'?

2) In 'My Last Duchess', how does Browning present the Duke's feelings as destructive?

3) What is the effect of reading 'A Complaint' as being about a friend rather than a lover?

4) What evidence is there in 'Love's Dog' that love can be complicated?

5) How does Armitage convey closeness between the couple in 'The Manhunt'?

6) Why do you think the poet uses unconventional imagery in 'i wanna be yours'?

Family Relationships

1) In 'Nettles', what is the effect of the speaker's reaction to their son's pain?

2) How is the lack of emotional connection between the speaker and their father shown in 'My Father Would Not Show Us'?

3) In 'One Flesh', how does the speaker feel about the changes to their parents' relationship? Give an example to support your answer.

Memory

1) How does the narrator's memory of the failed relationship in 'Neutral Tones' affect them in the present day?

2) What does the "unexploded mine" in 'The Manhunt' suggest about the soldier's memories?

3) In 'Nettles', how can you tell that painful events have happened again since the time in the poem?

Desire and Longing

1) How do you think the child in 'A Child to his Sick Grandfather' feels about the grandfather's illness and death? Explain your answer.

2) Summarise the Duke's feelings towards the Duchess in 'My Last Duchess'.

3) How is the knight's desire for the lady he meets shown in 'La Belle Dame Sans Merci'?

Practice Questions

Adoration

1) How is repetition used in 'Sonnet 43' to express the speaker's adoration of her lover?

2) In 'i wanna be yours', how does the speaker show their complete adoration of the other person?

3) Explain how the woman in 'She Walks in Beauty' is presented as perfect.

Death and Suffering

1) Explain the difference between the child's and the grandfather's suffering in 'A Child to his Sick Grandfather'.

2) In 'My Father Would Not Show Us', do you think the narrator's opinion of their father changes after his death? Explain your answer.

3) In 'Neutral Tones', how does Hardy use imagery to present the end of the relationship?

4) How are the potential negative aspects of a relationship expressed in the poem 'Valentine'?

5) Give three examples from 'La Belle Dame Sans Merci' that suggest that the knight is suffering.

6) In 'Nettles', how does the parent react to their child's suffering? Explain your answer.

Distance and Separation

1) What evidence is there in 'One Flesh' that the couple may not be as distant as they seem?

2) Describe how the poet creates a feeling of separation between the couple in 'First Date – She / First Date – He'.

3) Do you think the relationship between the two people in 'A Complaint' could be repaired? Give evidence to justify your answer.

Negative Emotions

1) Are the narrator's views towards love in 'Love's Dog' positive, negative, or balanced? Explain your answer.

2) Which details in 'Neutral Tones' indicate the narrator's feelings towards the other person?

3) In 'First Date – She / First Date – He', what evidence is there that the couple are nervous?

4) In 'One Flesh', how does Jennings create a sense of fear in the couple's relationship?

Practice Questions

It's no big secret — the best way to prepare for writing an essay in the exam is... by writing a practice essay. Here are five questions for you to have a crack at — don't forget to plan your answer before you start writing.

Exam-style Questions

1) Discuss the portrayal of distance between people in 'First Date – She / First Date – He' and one other poem from 'Relationships'.

2) Compare how death is presented in 'A Child to his Sick Grandfather' and one other poem from 'Relationships'.

3) Discuss how memory is presented in 'Neutral Tones' and one other poem from 'Relationships'.

4) 'Relationships change as people get older'.

   Using this quotation as a starting point, write about the theme of getting older in 'One Flesh' and one other poem from 'Relationships'.

5) Compare the ways feelings of bitterness are presented in 'Love's Dog' and one other poem from 'Relationships'.

Forms of Poetry

Form is about the rules poets follow when writing poetry. Like all good rules, they're there to be broken...

> 1) Form can be <u>rigid</u> and <u>regular</u> or <u>loose</u> and <u>irregular</u>.
> 2) Poets <u>choose</u> a form to create different <u>moods</u> and <u>effects</u>.

Some poems have a strict, regular form...

She Walks in Beauty (Pages 6-7)

1) The poem has a <u>rigid</u> form — it has three six-line stanzas with lines of similar length, and a <u>consistent</u> ABABAB rhyme scheme. The <u>regularity</u> of this form reflects the woman's <u>enduring beauty</u>.

2) The ABABAB rhyme scheme also emphasises how the woman's beauty is made up of a <u>contrast</u> between dark and light. These features <u>balance</u> each other out to produce her <u>perfect beauty</u>.

Sonnet 43 (Pages 12-13)

1) Barrett Browning's poem follows a strict <u>Petrarchan sonnet</u> form and is written in consistent <u>iambic pentameter</u>. This could imply that the speaker's feelings for her lover are <u>pure</u>.

2) Petrarchan sonnets often present a <u>problem</u> in the octave (the first eight lines), and then a <u>solution</u> in the sestet (the remaining six lines). 'Sonnet 43' <u>doesn't</u> do this, which suggests the speaker believes their love is <u>perfect</u> as it is — this reinforces the idea at the end of the poem that her love is <u>divine</u>.

La Belle Dame Sans Merci (Pages 2-3)

1) The poem is in <u>ballad</u> form, which is a form of poetry traditionally used to tell <u>folk stories</u>. By choosing this form, Keats could be trying to present the poem as a <u>timeless</u>, <u>ancient</u> story.

2) The poem is made up of <u>strict</u>, <u>regular</u> rhyming quatrains (<u>ABCB</u>) — this could indicate that the knight is <u>trapped</u> in his situation.

...whereas others are written in free verse

Valentine (Pages 18-19)

1) 'Valentine' is written in <u>free verse</u>, which gives the poem a <u>conversational</u> tone, as if the narrator is <u>speaking directly</u> to their lover, as well as to the reader.

2) It has short lines, and three of the poem's seven stanzas are only one line long. This <u>irregularity</u> suggests a <u>break away</u> from the <u>conventions</u> of more traditional love poetry and mirrors the way that the narrator <u>rejects</u> commonplace symbols of love, preferring to demonstrate love in their <u>own way</u>.

My Father Would Not Show Us (Pages 30-31)

1) The poem is written in <u>free verse</u>, with no fixed rhythm or rhyme scheme. This <u>irregularity</u> reflects how death and grief can't be ordered neatly — the <u>emotions</u> involved are <u>complicated</u>.

2) The poem begins with <u>short</u>, three-line stanzas, and the narrator speaks <u>concisely</u> ("It's cold in here"). The <u>stanzas then lengthen</u>, mirroring how the narrator begins to <u>respond emotionally</u> to the situation.

Other poems have regular forms...

The regular forms of 'First Date – She / First Date – He' could reflect the couple's overly analytical thoughts. In 'A Complaint', regular couplets indicate closeness between the speaker and the addressee.

Poetic Devices

Poets use lots of fancy techniques in their poems to make them as effective as possible. Here are just a few...

> 1) You need to be able to identify different techniques and make comparisons between them.
>
> 2) You should comment on the effect the technique has, as well as saying what it is.

Repetition can be used to support key ideas

Sonnet 43 (Pages 12-13)

1) Repetition of "I love thee" at the beginnings of lines (anaphora) emphasises the speaker's love.

2) The speaker loves the addressee to the "depth and breadth and height" her "soul can reach". This hyperbolic description uses the repetition of "and" to suggest her love is unlimited.

First Date – She / First Date – He (Pages 16-17)

1) Repetition between the two poems signals the similar thought processes and feelings of the two speakers. Although they struggle to connect with one another, their similar thoughts suggest that they're well-matched.

2) The line "And quite undistracted by me" appears in both poems. This repetition is ironic — each speaker thinks the other is "undistracted", but the repetition emphasises that both speakers are thinking about each other.

Brenda didn't know how to tell Jack that his singing was distracting the orchestra

Love's Dog (Pages 24-25)

1) The repetition of "What I love" / "What I hate" in 'Love's Dog' makes it seem as though the speaker is reciting a list. It increases the pace of the poem, creating a light-hearted, flippant tone.

2) This repetition has even more effect when the sequence is broken — "What I loathe about love" (line 13). This change shows the depth of the speaker's feelings and highlights a more serious dislike.

i wanna be yours (Pages 22-23)

1) The repetition of "let me be your" suggests that the narrator is pleading with someone. They are trying to announce their desire to be with someone, but this repetition could hint at desperation.

2) Repeating "i wanna be yours" at the end of each stanza acts as a refrain, ensuring that the focus of the poem remains on the narrator's aim of belonging to the other person.

Enjambment can offer clues about the characters

The Manhunt (Pages 28-29)

1) The poem is split into couplet-length stanzas, most of which have an enjambed first line and an end-stopped second line. This creates a faltering rhythm that reflects the wife's slow progress.

2) The enjambment between the final three stanzas of the poem hints that the distance between the couple may not be permanent, and could symbolise the barriers between the couple breaking down.

My Last Duchess (Pages 14-15)

1) The rigid rhyming couplets in the poem show the Duke's need for control, but enjambment between the couplets makes the poem seem less strictly regulated.

2) This could hint at how unstable the Duke is — although he tries to control the people around him, his jealousy and need for power have made him unbalanced.

Poetic Devices

Punctuation affects the pace and tone of a poem

Valentine (Pages 18-19)

1) Frequent full stops give the poem an uncomfortable, disjointed rhythm, which could hint at the disruption and discomfort love can cause.

2) End-stopping in the final stanza keeps each line neatly contained, which could echo the "possessive" aspect of love.

3) The word "Lethal." (line 21) is end-stopped and sits alone on a line. The end-stopping is abrupt, highlighting the poem's message that love can be dangerous and brutal.

A Complaint (Pages 8-9)

1) Caesurae disrupt the poem's rhythm, e.g. in "I trust it is, — and never dry". These make the narrator's thought processes seem fragmented, which emphasises their intense, overwhelming emotions.

2) Exclamation marks in the second stanza express the narrator's joy in the past and create a pause in the poem, indicating that the narrator is stopping to reflect on these "happy moments".

3) Rhetorical questions, e.g. "What have I?", create a thoughtful tone. This emphasises that the narrator is dwelling on thoughts of their lost relationship.

One Flesh (Pages 20-21)

1) The caesura in line 1 separates the two clauses about the couple "Lying apart", reflecting the separation between them. However, the phrases are separated by a comma, rather than a full stop, perhaps indicating that they aren't completely separate, and there is still some love between them.

2) Caesurae throughout the rest of the poem, e.g. "How cool they lie. They hardly ever touch", further emphasise the distance between them. These frequent pauses also slow the pace of the poem, indicating the couple's strained relationship.

Dramatic irony can reveal what the characters don't

First Date – She / First Date – He (Pages 16-17)

1) The two poems have different speakers, so the reader is aware of what both speakers are privately thinking ("I was thrilled", "she is very attractive"). This makes their mutual interest clear.

2) The speakers think they "see" what's going on, but dramatic irony allows the reader to recognise that their assumptions that they are "quite undistracted" by each other are wrong.

My Last Duchess (Pages 14-15)

1) There is a difference between what the Duke shares and what the reader can work out from his narrative — his words are innocent, but they often have a sinister meaning.

2) Subtle but threatening references to death, e.g. the "Half-flush that dies along her throat", indicate the Duke's malevolence. As a result, although the description of the former Duchess's death is indirect ("all smiles stopped together"), the reader works out that his "commands" were to have her killed.

Language helps the reader to connect...

In 'My Father Would Not Show Us', the poet uses sensory language to create vivid memories of the past. 'Nettles' uses emotive language to show the reader the parent's anger and the child's pain.

Imagery

Imagery is language that creates a picture — it includes similes, metaphors and personification.

1) Imagery is often used to make descriptions more vivid or powerful.

2) It can also provide powerful contrasts to traditional ideas.

Imagery can be powerful...

Nettles (Pages 26-27)

1) An extended metaphor describes the nettles as soldiers — they form a "regiment of spite" which attacks the child. The comparison to soldiers makes the nettles seem fierce and disciplined.

2) The nettles are personified as "recruits" that have been "called up", which portrays the attack on the child as a deliberate effort to cause him harm. The personification suggests that the nettles can think for themselves as if they were human, emphasising how dangerous they are to the child.

3) The contrast between the military imagery and the child "seeking comfort" highlights the child's innocence and vulnerability.

The Manhunt (Pages 28-29)

1) Metaphors to do with inanimate objects describe the man's war-damaged body. For example, the narrator refers to "the rungs of his broken ribs", emphasising the dehumanising nature of war.

2) The "sweating, unexploded mine / buried deep in his mind" is a metaphor that hints at the man's distress, suggesting that war has left him with unresolved emotional issues that he still needs to tackle.

...and sometimes unconventional

She Walks in Beauty (Pages 6-7)

1) The unconventional simile comparing the lady in the poem to "the night" in line 1 contrasts with traditional romantic imagery, which often references light and brightness. This unusual comparison suggests that the woman's difference makes her perfect — she stands out from other women.

2) The poem goes on to include light imagery as well ("all that's best of dark and bright") — this suggests that the woman is beautiful in a conventionally romantic way too.

i wanna be yours (Pages 22-23)

1) The narrator uses imagery of mundane items to demonstrate their love, such as a "coffee pot" and an "electric heater". This indicates their desire to be part of someone's daily life, but could potentially be seen as comical or even insincere.

2) Day-to-day imagery is unconventional in love poetry, which often uses noble and grand imagery — this could suggest that the narrator's "deep devotion" extends beyond the traditional to all aspects of love and relationships.

Valentine (Pages 18-19)

1) Duffy uses the onion as an extended metaphor for the narrator and their lover's relationship. This imagery presents their love as unsentimental and unusual.

2) The simile "like the careful undressing of love" suggests that by accepting the metaphorical onion and thinking carefully about what it represents, the addressee will come to understand love better.

Section Three — Poetic Techniques

Imagery

Water imagery can convey a character's emotions

A Complaint (Pages 8-9)

1) The metaphor describing the addressee's love as a "<u>fountain</u>" reveals how the narrator <u>treasures</u> the love they shared — fountains are lively and often something to be <u>admired</u>. This comparison indicates the <u>joy</u> and <u>energy</u> the love provided.

2) The impact of the "<u>change</u>" transforms the "fountain" of love into a "<u>well</u>" which indicates the extent of the <u>loss</u> that the narrator feels. Water in a well is <u>inactive</u>, dull and <u>buried</u> deep underground, indicating how the nature of their love has <u>changed</u>.

Neutral Tones (Pages 10-11)

1) The poem uses the repeated image of a <u>pond</u> in "<u>winter</u>", which is "edged with grayish leaves". The <u>colourless</u>, <u>bleak</u> setting creates a <u>pessimistic</u> mood which reflects the narrator's <u>attitude</u>.

2) A "pond" has <u>no current</u> — the water in it is <u>still</u> and <u>lifeless</u>, reflecting the lifelessness of the narrator's <u>relationship</u>.

3) The image of the pond appears at the <u>beginning</u> and <u>end</u> of the poem, emphasising that this is the moment which returns to <u>haunt</u> the narrator after other bad experiences have confirmed to them that "love deceives".

Neil had found an easier way to convey his emotions

Imagery can be used to highlight contrasting themes

One Flesh (Pages 20-21)

1) The simile in line 7 ("<u>Tossed up like flotsam</u>") suggests that the couple were <u>powerless</u> to avoid their situation. The <u>comparison</u> to the <u>wreckage</u> of a destroyed ship suggests that the <u>end</u> of their "former passion" has been <u>difficult</u> and <u>destructive</u>.

2) Despite the changes that have happened, the narrator's description of <u>time</u> as a "feather" <u>softens</u> the mood and implies that some <u>changes</u> have happened <u>gently</u>, without the couple's knowledge.

Love's Dog (Pages 24-25)

1) The speaker uses a series of images to convey their <u>opinion</u> about the <u>positives</u> and <u>negatives</u> of love.

2) Positive ideas about love in the poem are often conveyed through imagery to do with <u>animals</u>, e.g. a "<u>petting zoo</u>" and a "<u>zookeeper</u>". This imagery evokes the idea of <u>protection</u> and <u>care</u>, and indicates the <u>loving</u> aspects of a relationship.

3) However, the image of the "<u>sick parrot</u>" could indicate that even the positive sides of love can <u>become negative</u>. The speaker is pointing out that even the <u>good things</u> in a relationship have the potential to <u>go wrong</u>.

OTHER POEMS

Other poems use personification...

Hardy personifies the "starving sod" in 'Neutral Tones' to create an impression of suffering and death. The "weary fire" in 'A Child to his Sick Grandfather' is personified to represent the ageing grandfather.

Use of Sound

Poems are often intended to be read aloud, so the sounds that words make are particularly important.

> 1) Sounds can be <u>powerful</u> in poetry and can have a <u>positive</u> or <u>negative</u> effect.
> 2) Certain letters sound <u>harsh</u> and <u>bitter</u>, whilst others sound <u>light</u> and <u>joyful</u>.

Sounds can convey positive ideas...

She Walks in Beauty (Pages 6-7)

1) The <u>alliteration</u> in "<u>c</u>loudless <u>c</u>limes and <u>s</u>tarry <u>s</u>kies" is <u>delicate</u>, reflecting the lady's <u>elegant beauty</u>.

2) <u>Assonant vowel sounds</u> elongate words (e.g. the '<u>a</u>' in "gr<u>a</u>ce", "w<u>a</u>ves" and "r<u>a</u>ven") showing the speaker's <u>appreciation</u> of the lady and giving the impression they are taking their <u>time</u> to <u>admire</u> her.

A Complaint (Pages 8-9)

1) The <u>alliteration</u> of the '<u>f</u>' sound in "<u>f</u>ountain", "<u>f</u>ond" and "<u>f</u>low" in the first stanza flows from <u>line to line</u>, mimicking the flow of <u>water</u> and emphasising the <u>force</u> of the love the speaker felt.

2) Repeated plosive '<u>b</u>' sounds in the second stanza ("<u>B</u>lest" and "<u>b</u>liss") give the poem a <u>lively</u> tone. They draw attention to the speaker's <u>excitement</u> when they recall the <u>happy memories</u> they shared with the other person.

...or they can suggest something negative

Nettles (Pages 26-27)

1) The poem uses <u>sibilance</u> in "<u>s</u>pite behind the <u>sh</u>ed" to make the nettles seem <u>sinister</u> and <u>threatening</u>.

2) Alliterative '<u>b</u>' sounds in the poem are used to show the strength of the parent's <u>anger</u> and the child's <u>pain</u>. The phrase "<u>b</u>listers <u>b</u>eaded" sounds <u>aggressive</u> and highlights the child's <u>pain</u>, while the <u>harsh plosive</u> sounds in "<u>b</u>illhook" and "<u>b</u>lade" give an indication of the parent's <u>fury</u>.

Valentine (Pages 18-19)

1) In 'Valentine', <u>alliteration</u> is used to emphasise the narrator's <u>disdain</u> for romantic <u>clichés</u>.

2) The phrase "<u>red rose</u>" is <u>monosyllabic</u> and the alliteration sounds <u>dull</u> and <u>lifeless</u> — this perhaps shows how <u>uninterested</u> the speaker is in the <u>traditional</u> expression of <u>love</u> it represents.

3) In "<u>cute card or a kissogram</u>", the 'c' and 'k' sounds are <u>harsh</u> and indicate the speaker's <u>contempt</u> for <u>traditional</u>, "<u>cute</u>" Valentine's gifts. This could be because the speaker thinks traditional gifts are <u>dishonest</u>, in contrast to their own "truthful" approach.

Love's Dog (Pages 24-25)

1) The final two stanzas are heavily <u>alliterative</u>, using <u>plosive</u> '<u>b</u>' and '<u>p</u>' sounds to emphasise the <u>strength</u> of the narrator's <u>emotions</u>.

2) The <u>blunt</u> sounds in "<u>b</u>oil-wash" and "<u>b</u>urnt toast and <u>b</u>onemeal" highlight the narrator's <u>bitterness</u> and <u>resentment</u> of these things — they "<u>hate</u>" and "<u>loathe</u>" them respectively.

Other poems also use alliteration...

In 'My Father Would Not Show Us', alliteration in the first stanza creates dull, heavy sounds. Alliteration in 'Sonnet 43' emphasises the speaker's simple and passionate love, e.g. "purely", "Praise" and "passion".

Rhyme and Rhythm

Rejoice happily, your teacher has marshmallows — there's no excuse for spelling 'rhythm' wrong in the exam.

> 1) Rhyme and rhythm often emphasise the main messages or ideas in a poem.
> 2) They can also affect the mood and pace of a poem.

Rhyme can reinforce ideas in the poem

A Complaint (Pages 8-9)

1) The poem uses strong rhymes — stressed vowels and their following sounds usually match identically (e.g. "count" and "fount"). This could show the strength of the speaker's emotions.

2) The rhyming couplet at the end of each stanza could indicate the close connection between the speaker and the addressee. Even when speaker reveals the extent of their loss, the strong rhyme in the couplet remains — their feelings haven't changed.

Neutral Tones (Pages 10-11)

1) The ABBA rhyme scheme mirrors the cyclical structure of the poem — just as the poem begins and ends with the image of the pond, the 'A' rhyme returns at the end of each stanza. This reflects the way that the narrator's memory of the break-up returns to affect him.

2) Most of the rhyming words are monosyllabic, e.g. "day" / "gray" and "God" / "sod". This creates a deadening effect at the end of each line, which emphasises the passionless tone of the poem.

My Last Duchess (Pages 14-15)

1) Rhyming couplets are used throughout the poem to help create a rigid form — this shows how the Duke controls the poem, just as he controlled his wife's fate.

2) The regularity of the rhymes also mirrors the Duke's stubborn, unwavering character — the rhyme scheme allows no space for change or questioning, just as the Duke chooses "Never to stoop".

A poem's rhythm affects its pace and mood

La Belle Dame Sans Merci (Pages 2-3)

1) Iambic tetrameter in the first three lines of each stanza gives the poem a steady rhythm. This rhythm is typical of ballads and makes it sound as though a traditional story is being narrated.

2) Shorter last lines in each stanza cut the rhythm short, reflecting the shortening of the knight's time with the lady. Each stanza's abrupt ending unsettles the mood and highlights the knight's despair.

Nettles (Pages 26-27)

1) 'Nettles' has a steady, relentless iambic pentameter rhythm, which echoes the regularity of marching soldiers. It could also represent a heart beating, indicating the parent's powerful love for the child.

2) The regular rhythm is broken in line 10, which has an extra syllable. This calls attention to the parent's frantic and overwhelming desire to protect their son in this part of the poem.

Poems may not have a regular rhyme scheme...

'Valentine' has no rhyme scheme, which creates an unsettling mood and reflects the speaker's attempt to avoid convention. The irregular rhyme scheme in 'Love's Dog' reflects the unpredictability of love.

Voice

The voice is a key feature of a poem — it can have a big effect on how the poet's message is conveyed.

> 1) A first-person voice gives you one person's perspective.
> 2) Poetry can use conversational language to hint at the speaker's character.

Using a first-person narrator makes the poem more personal

i wanna be yours (Pages 22-23)

1) The first-person voice allows the narrator to clearly communicate their personal desires — the repetition of "me" and "i" stresses how emotionally involved they are in the situation.

2) Although the first-person narrative is one-sided, the repeated use of second-person pronouns ("your", "yours", "you") ensures that the narrator's focus on the other person is clear.

My Father Would Not Show Us (Pages 30-31)

1) A first-person voice allows the reader to see the speaker's private thoughts about their father's death.

2) The speaker's thoughts return to images of their father's absence as he "hid" and "turned" away. This suggests that they're dwelling on these thoughts and regret not having a closer relationship.

First Date – She / First Date – He (Pages 16-17)

1) The use of a different first-person voice in each poem allows the reader to see the same event from two different perspectives. Both speakers reveal their private feelings and thoughts, e.g. "I was thrilled", "I'm a bit nervous".

2) The separate narrative voices highlight the inconsistencies between what the speakers think is happening and reality, and emphasise that each speaker is so focused on their own perspective that they don't recognise the true thoughts and feelings of the other.

Poems can include conversational language

A Child to his Sick Grandfather (Pages 4-5)

1) The child addresses their grandfather directly, calling him "dad" — this abbreviation of "Grand-dad" is affectionate and highlights how relaxed the child is around him.

2) Informal language (e.g. "I am right glad") makes the poem feel personal and portrays the child's youth.

3) The child asks for reassurance from their grandfather, e.g. "You will not die and leave us then?" This shows that they rely on his opinions and thoughts, and highlights how lost they will be after his death.

My Last Duchess (Pages 14-15)

1) The poem is written entirely in the Duke's voice. Interjections, e.g. "how shall I say?", and contractions, e.g. "'twas" and "Will't", give the sense that the Duke is speaking aloud.

2) Questions ("Will't please you rise?") and references to "Sir" show that the Duke is talking to someone. However, we only ever hear the Duke's voice, which emphasises his power and need for control.

Some poems use direct address...

The speakers in 'Valentine' and 'Sonnet 43' address their lovers directly, giving the poems a personal tone. In 'Neutral Tones', direct address reflects the speaker's continuing bitterness towards their ex-lover.

Beginnings of Poems

Poets know that first impressions are important, so there's usually something to say about a poem's start.

> 1) The beginning of a poem often <u>sets the tone</u> for the rest of the poem.
>
> 2) Poets aim to <u>draw in</u> their readers, and to establish something of the poem's <u>meaning</u>.

Some beginnings introduce questions to be answered...

La Belle Dame Sans Merci (Pages 2-3)

1) An <u>anonymous speaker</u> introduces the knight in the poem, and <u>questions</u> what might "ail" him.

2) The knight is described as <u>pale</u> and <u>unwell</u>, so it is clear that something has happened to him. This engages the reader's attention for the rest of the story, in which he <u>explains</u> what has happened.

Sonnet 43 (Pages 12-13)

1) The speaker's <u>opening question</u> ("How do I love thee?") is <u>rhetorical</u>. It is used to introduce the rest of the poem, as the speaker goes on to "<u>count the ways</u>" they love the addressee.

2) This <u>logical</u> structure emphasises the speaker's <u>methodical</u> consideration of every aspect of their love.

...while others set the tone

Neutral Tones (Pages 10-11)

1) The <u>setting</u> of the "<u>pond</u>" on a "<u>winter day</u>" is established immediately. This creates a powerful image of a <u>cold</u>, <u>desolate</u> scene.

2) The narrator and his lover "<u>stood</u>" by the pond — their <u>inactivity</u> helps to establish the <u>lifeless atmosphere</u> that characterises the poem.

3) The words in line 1 are <u>simple</u> and mostly <u>monosyllabic</u>. This creates a <u>deadening</u> effect, which hints at the narrator's <u>grief</u> and sets up the '<u>neutral</u>' tone of the poem.

"We frolicked by a pond that summer day..."

One Flesh (Pages 20-21)

1) The description of the couple as "<u>apart</u>" and "<u>separate</u>" in the first line immediately establishes <u>distance</u>. The following <u>descriptions</u> of each half of the couple are on <u>separate lines</u>, which deepens the sense of <u>separation</u>.

2) The <u>opening line</u> also suggests that the <u>distance</u> between the couple hasn't always been present — they are "<u>apart now</u>", implying that they were <u>once together</u>.

Valentine (Pages 18-19)

1) The first line makes it <u>clear</u> that the poem is <u>not</u> a <u>traditional</u> love poem. The opening word is strongly negative ("<u>Not</u>"), which shows that the speaker does not want to be associated with the usual <u>clichés</u> of a "red rose" or "satin heart".

2) The speaker then immediately offers something else in line 2, "<u>an onion</u>" — this <u>unexpected</u> gift <u>contrasts</u> with those mentioned in the first line, emphasising that the speaker's love is <u>different</u>.

OTHER POEMS

You could write about the beginning of any poem...

The opening lines of 'A Complaint', 'Nettles' and 'My Last Duchess' all introduce a significant idea or scenario that the reader wants to know more about — e.g. the intriguing "change" in 'A Complaint'.

Endings of Poems

Relief might be your emotion when you reach the end of a poem, but please don't write that in your exam...

> 1) Last lines often <u>sum up</u> or neatly <u>round off</u> a poem.
> 2) Sometimes endings can leave the reader with <u>questions</u> or <u>doubts</u>.

Endings can create a sense of finality...

My Father Would Not Show Us (Pages 30-31)

1) <u>Despite</u> the narrator's growing <u>understanding</u> of their father's behaviour, the poem <u>ends</u> with an image of the father with his "<u>face to the wall</u>". This heightens the sense of <u>sadness</u> in the poem, as it is now <u>too late</u> for anything to change.

2) The <u>last clause</u> reinforces the <u>finality</u> of the situation — "<u>he lay</u>" is <u>separated</u> from the rest of the line by a comma, reflecting how the father's <u>death</u>, and his <u>separation</u> from his children, cannot be changed.

My Last Duchess (Pages 14-15)

1) The <u>focus</u> at the end <u>shifts</u> back to the Duke's <u>art collection</u>. He points out his statue of "<u>Neptune</u>", boasting that "<u>Claus of Innsbruck</u>" made it for him — this shows his <u>pride</u> and <u>vanity</u>.

2) This confirms that, <u>for the Duke</u>, the <u>story</u> of his last Duchess is <u>over</u> — he has <u>moved on</u> and she is now just another <u>possession</u> in his art collection.

...or they can be ambiguous

The Manhunt (Pages 28-29)

1) The last line shows the couple's <u>progress</u>, as they have come "<u>close</u>" to one another. However, it also suggests they haven't <u>fully reconnected</u>, leaving the reader <u>uncertain</u> about their future.

2) This idea is emphasised through the way "close" <u>almost rhymes</u> with the previous line ("<u>closed</u>") — the poem's <u>fractured rhyme scheme</u> hints that war has <u>damaged</u> their sense of <u>togetherness</u>.

A Child to his Sick Grandfather (Pages 4-5)

1) At the end of the poem, the child says that their grandfather can no longer "<u>hear</u>" them. Although it is <u>heavily implied</u> that the grandfather has died, the child does not state this directly, perhaps suggesting that they are <u>naive</u> or <u>lack understanding</u>.

2) The final couplet ends with a <u>half-rhyme</u> ("head" / "dad") — the <u>full rhyme</u> would be '<u>dead</u>'. This emphasises the reader's <u>impression</u> that the grandfather is dead.

A Complaint (Pages 8-9)

1) The final stanza <u>repeats</u> words from the first stanza (e.g. "change", "poor"). This creates a <u>cyclical</u> structure, which implies that the narrator's situation is <u>fixed</u> — the "change" <u>cannot</u> be <u>reversed</u>.

2) However, the narrator's <u>belief</u> that the "well of <u>love</u>" is "never dry" shows that there may be <u>hope</u> — even in the <u>final line</u> of the poem, their heart is still "<u>fond</u>".

Other poems can also leave the reader with questions...

'First Date — She / First Date – He' and 'La Belle Dame Sans Merci' leave the reader with questions to be answered. It is unclear what will happen next for the couple, or if the knight will ever escape the hillside.

Section Three — Poetic Techniques

Practice Questions

It's the end of the section and yep, you guessed it — time for some questions to check if you've taken everything in. Try to answer them without looking back through the section — that's the best way to see if you're on the way to being a poetry pro.

Forms of Poetry

1) Explain how the form of 'She Walks in Beauty' is used to illustrate the woman's attractiveness.

2) Comment on the form of 'Sonnet 43'. Why might the poet have chosen this form?

3) In 'Valentine', how does Duffy use form to present the narrator's emotions?

Poetic Devices

1) How is anaphora used in 'Sonnet 43' to highlight the narrator's ideas?

2) In 'Love's Dog', what is the effect of repetition on the poem's tone?

3) Explain the effect of the enjambment in 'The Manhunt'.

4) How does the use of punctuation in 'A Complaint' affect the reader's perception of the narrator?

5) What effect do the caesurae in 'One Flesh' have on the reader's understanding of the couple's relationship?

6) Describe how dramatic irony is used in 'First Date – She / First Date – He'.

Imagery

1) Do you think the use of extended metaphor is more effective in 'Nettles' or 'A Complaint'? Explain your answer.

2) Find an example of imagery used in 'The Manhunt' to describe the soldier's body. Explain the meaning and significance of the image.

3) Find a metaphor or simile used to describe the woman in 'She Walks in Beauty'. Explain what this shows about the narrator's feelings towards her.

4) How is imagery used in 'Valentine' to present the complicated nature of love?

5) How does Hardy use imagery to convey the narrator's pessimism in 'Neutral Tones'?

6) How are similes used in 'One Flesh' to show how the relationship between the couple has changed?

Practice Questions

Use of Sound

1) Find an example of assonance in 'She Walks in Beauty' and explain its effect.

2) Find two examples of alliteration in 'Nettles' with different effects.
Explain how and why they are different.

3) How is sound used to convey the narrator's feelings in 'Love's Dog'?

Rhyme and Rhythm

1) Describe the effect of the rhyming couplets used in 'My Last Duchess'.

2) How does the rhythm in 'La Belle Dame Sans Merci' affect the mood of the poem?

3) Explain the effect of the change in rhythm in 'Nettles'.

Voice

1) Why do you think the poet of 'First Date – She / First Date – He' chose to use two first-person narrators?

2) Why do you think Cooper Clarke chose to use direct address in 'i wanna be yours'?

3) In 'My Last Duchess', how does Browning create the impression of a conversation taking place?

Beginnings of Poems

1) How does the opening of 'Sonnet 43' draw the reader into the poem?

2) What does the beginning of 'One Flesh' suggest about the couple's relationship?

3) Choose a poem not mentioned on page 57 and write about the effect of its opening.

Endings of Poems

1) How does the poet convey a sense of finality at the end of 'My Father Would Not Show Us'?

2) Explain what the ending of 'The Manhunt' suggests about the relationship between the couple.

3) Describe how the ending of 'A Child to his Sick Grandfather' reflects the narrator's young age.

Practice Questions

Here's your third and final batch of exam-style questions. Sections Four and Five have lots of handy advice about writing great exam answers, so have a read of those pages if you're looking for some hints and tips.

You should discuss the form, structure and language used by the poets and the effects that these create. It's also important that you include relevant information about the contexts surrounding the poems — you could discuss how historical events or culture may have influenced the poets.

Exam-style Questions

1) Compare how the poets present suffering in 'Nettles' and one other poem from 'Relationships'.

2) Explore the ways romantic love is presented in 'i wanna be yours' and one other poem from 'Relationships'.

3) Explore how love is presented as destructive in 'My Last Duchess' and one other poem from 'Relationships'.

4) Compare how imagery is used in 'She Walks in Beauty' and one other poem from 'Relationships'.

5) With reference to 'Sonnet 43' and one other poem from 'Relationships', discuss how adoration is presented.

The Poetry Exam

For your Edexcel English Literature course, you'll have to sit two exams — Paper 1 and Paper 2. This book will help you prepare for the Poetry Anthology section, which is part of Paper 2.

This is how your Paper 2 exam will work

1) The Paper 2 exam lasts for 2 hours and 15 minutes. It will be split into three parts, like this:

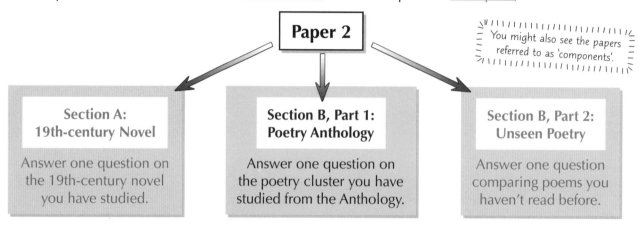

Paper 2

You might also see the papers referred to as 'components'.

Section A:
19th-century Novel
Answer one question on the 19th-century novel you have studied.

Section B, Part 1:
Poetry Anthology
Answer one question on the poetry cluster you have studied from the Anthology.

Section B, Part 2:
Unseen Poetry
Answer one question comparing poems you haven't read before.

2) The next few pages give you tips on how to answer the question in Section B, Part 1.

3) Section B, Part 1 has one question about each poetry cluster. You should only answer one of these questions — make sure you answer the question on the 'Relationships' cluster.

4) Section B, Part 1 is worth 20 marks, which is about 12.5% of your entire GCSE. In the exam, you should spend about 35 minutes on Section B, Part 1.

5) You're not allowed to take your own anthology or any notes about the poems into the exam.

Read the question carefully and underline key words

1) Read the question for 'Relationships' carefully. Underline the theme and any other key words.

2) The question will give you one poem and ask you to compare it with any other poem from the same cluster. You'll be given a list of all the poems to help you choose — pick one that relates to the theme.

3) Here's the kind of question you'll get in the exam:

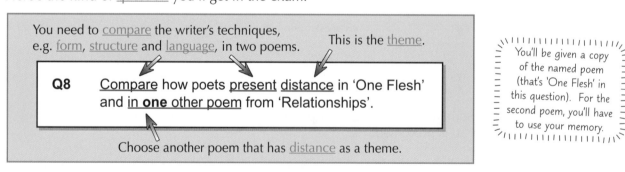

You need to compare the writer's techniques, e.g. form, structure and language, in two poems.   This is the theme.

Q8   Compare how poets present distance in 'One Flesh' and in **one** other poem from 'Relationships'.

Choose another poem that has distance as a theme.

You'll be given a copy of the named poem (that's 'One Flesh' in this question). For the second poem, you'll have to use your memory.

There are three main ways to get marks

There are three main things to keep in mind when you're planning and writing your answer:

- Give your own thoughts and opinions on the poems and support them with quotes from the text.
- Explain the effects of features like form, structure and language.
- Describe the similarities and differences between poems and their contexts.

How to Structure Your Answer

A solid structure is essential — it lets the examiner follow your argument nice and easily. The best way to make sure you write a well-structured essay in the exam is to make a plan before you start writing (see p.67).

Start with an introduction and end with a conclusion

1) Your introduction should begin by giving a clear answer to the question in a sentence or two. Use the rest of the introduction to briefly develop this idea — try to include some of the main ideas from your plan.

2) The main body of your essay should be three to five paragraphs that compare the two poems.

3) Finish your essay with a conclusion — this should summarise your answer to the question. It's also your last chance to impress the examiner, so try to make your final sentence memorable.

Compare the poems throughout your essay

1) In each paragraph of the main body, write about one poem and then explain whether the other poem is similar or different. Don't just write several paragraphs about one poem, followed by several paragraphs about the other.

Remember to start a new paragraph every time you start comparing a new feature of the poems.

2) Every paragraph should compare a feature of the poems, such as their form, their structure, the language they use or the feelings they put across.

3) Link your ideas with words like 'similarly', 'likewise' or 'equally' when you're writing about a similarity. Or use phrases such as 'in contrast' and 'on the other hand' if you're explaining a difference.

Use P.E.E.D. to structure each paragraph

1) P.E.E.D. stands for: Point, Example, Explain, Develop.

POINT — Begin each paragraph by making a comparison between the two poems.

EXAMPLE — Then give an example from one of the poems.

EXPLAIN — Explain how the example supports your opening point.

After you've explained your first example, give an example from the other poem and explain that too.

DEVELOP — Develop your point by writing about its effect on the reader, how it links to another part of the poem, how it relates to the poem's context, or by adding to the comparison with the other poem.

2) This is just a framework to make sure your paragraphs have all the features they need to pick up marks — you don't have to follow it rigidly in every paragraph.

3) Here's an example of how you could use P.E.E.D. to structure a paragraph:

Start with a point that compares the two poems.

Explain how the examples relate to your opening point.

'Sonnet 43' and 'Love's Dog' both use anaphora to express key ideas about love. In 'Sonnet 43', several lines begin with the phrase "I love thee", which emphasises the strength of the speaker's affection. This also draws attention to the words that follow, e.g. "purely", which state all the ways she loves the subject, helping the reader understand the extent of her love. Similarly, the speaker of 'Love's Dog' uses the repeated phrase "What I" at the start of lines, but then varies between describing what they "love" and "hate" about love. The anaphora draws attention to the extremes of emotion that love can cause. The lack of a pattern in whether "love" or "hate" follows the anaphora gives the reader the impression that love can be unpredictable.

Give examples from both poems.

You can develop your point separately for each poem, or write about both poems at the same time.

Section Four — Exam Advice

How to Answer the Question

The exam is no time to discover your inner politician — you do need to answer the question you're given.

Look closely at language, form and structure

1) To get top marks, you need to pay close attention to the techniques the poets use.

2) Analyse the form and structure of the poems, which includes their rhyme scheme and rhythm.

3) Explore language — think about why the poets have used certain words and language techniques.

4) You also need to comment on the effect that these techniques have on the reader. The examiner wants to hear what you think of a poem and how it makes you feel.

5) This is the kind of thing you could write about language:

> 'The Manhunt' uses a combination of violent sounds and language of fragility to convey the man's broken state. The metaphor of the "parachute silk of his punctured lung" uses alliteration of the plosive 'p' sound to add a stabbing force to the phrase, emphasising how his lung has been damaged in the war. The man's fragility is reinforced through the use of the delicate material "silk", which could suggest that he is not as strong as he was, or that humans are not designed to be placed in such dangerous situations. The fact that the narrator describes the soldier's body as a series of individual, damaged body parts further emphasises the soldier's broken state.

Analyse the effect of key quotes.

Always develop your ideas.

Always support your ideas with details from the text

1) To get top marks, you need to back up your ideas with quotes from or references to the text.

2) Choose your quotes carefully — they have to be relevant to the point you're making.

3) Don't quote large chunks of text — instead, use short quotes and embed them in your sentences.

✗ In 'My Last Duchess', the Duke seems uncertain of his wife's faithfulness — he says "She had / A heart – how shall I say? – too soon made glad, / Too easily impressed; she liked whate'er / She looked on, and her looks went everywhere."

This quote is too long and it doesn't fit into the sentence structure.

✓ The Duke in 'My Last Duchess' hints that his wife was unfaithful by describing how she liked "whate'er / She looked on" and claiming that she looked "everywhere".

These quotes are nicely embedded into the sentence.

4) Don't forget to explain your quotes — you need to use them as evidence to support your argument.

✗ The narrator in 'A Child to his Sick Grandfather' describes how their grandfather looks physically. They describe how his beard is "lank and thin", how the "white hairs" on his head are "Scant", and how his cheeks have become "wan and hollow".

This just repeats what is said in the poem.

✓ In 'A Child to his Sick Grandfather', the narrator uses language to highlight how close their grandfather is to dying. Adjectives such as "thin", "Scant" and "hollow" emphasise the reduction in his physicality as well as his increased frailty. The word "hollow" also implies an emptiness, as though part of the grandfather is now missing.

This explains how the quotes support the argument.

How to Answer the Question

The examiner doesn't have a list of right and wrong answers for this exam — you'll get plenty of marks for original or creative interpretations, as long as they're relevant and your points are developed well.

Give alternative interpretations

1) You need to show you're aware that poems can be interpreted in more than one way.

2) If a poem is a bit ambiguous, or you think that a particular line or phrase could have several different meanings, then say so.

> The speaker in 'Valentine' suggests that they are willing to commit to their lover. They describe how the strong taste of the onion will linger and "stay" on their lover's lips, and explain that they too will stay "faithful". The description of the onion's potent taste powerfully conveys the strength of the speaker's love to the reader. However, the use of the adjectives "fierce" and "possessive" to describe the "kiss" of the onion also hints at a sinister undercurrent in the relationship, implying that the speaker's desire to stay is so strong that it has become dangerously obsessive.

Remember to support your interpretations with evidence from the poem.

3) Be original with your ideas — just make sure you can back them up with an example from the text.

Show some wider knowledge

1) It's important to explain how the ideas in the poems relate to their context.

2) When you're thinking about a particular poem, consider these aspects of context:

Biographical — Is the poet drawing on events or experiences in their life?
Historical — Do the ideas in the poem relate to the time in which it's written or set?
Geographical — How is the poem shaped and influenced by the place in which it's set?
Social — Is the poet criticising or praising the society or community they're writing about?
Cultural — Does the poet draw on a particular aspect of their background or culture?
Literary — Was the poet influenced by other works of literature or a particular literary movement?

3) Here are a couple of examples of how you might use context in your answer:

> It's thought that Wordsworth wrote 'A Complaint' about his friend, Samuel Taylor Coleridge, who had become addicted to the drug opium and grown reclusive. The "silence and obscurity" in the poem may refer to the breakdown of their friendship. If this is the case, then Wordsworth reveals how the love between friends can be just as powerful as romantic love — indeed, it is hard to tell what kind of relationship the speaker mourns, as it is never explicitly stated.

> 'La Belle Dame Sans Merci' may be indicative of Keats's despair following the death of his brother, Thomas, from tuberculosis in 1818. The knight is "haggard" and "palely loitering", which may mirror the deterioration of his brother's health and physical state, or reflect how Keats was in the early stages of the illness himself at the time the poem was written.

How to Answer the Question

It's not just what you write that gets you a top grade — it's how you write it. Your writing style should be clear and you need to use the correct terms to show the examiner you know what you're talking about.

Use sophisticated language

1) Your writing has to sound <u>sophisticated</u> and <u>precise</u>.

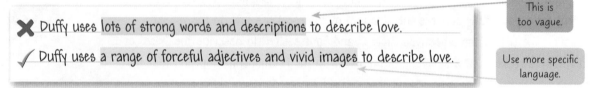

✗ In 'Love's Dog', Hadfield gives lots of examples to look at the two different sides of love. ← *Not very sophisticated.*

✓ In 'Love's Dog', Hadfield presents a range of parallels that explore the dual nature of love. ← *This sounds much better.*

2) It should be <u>concise</u> and <u>accurate</u>, with no <u>vague words</u> or <u>waffle</u>.

✗ Duffy uses lots of strong words and descriptions to describe love. ← *This is too vague.*

✓ Duffy uses a range of forceful adjectives and vivid images to describe love. ← *Use more specific language.*

3) Your writing should also show an <u>impressive range</u> of <u>vocabulary</u>.

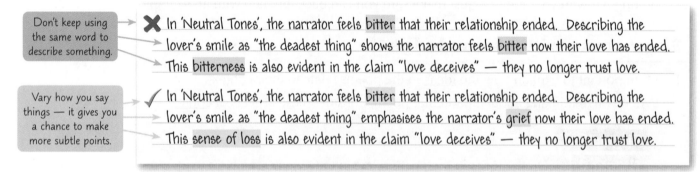

Don't keep using the same word to describe something.

✗ In 'Neutral Tones', the narrator feels bitter that their relationship ended. Describing the lover's smile as "the deadest thing" shows the narrator feels bitter now their love has ended. This bitterness is also evident in the claim "love deceives" — they no longer trust love.

Vary how you say things — it gives you a chance to make more subtle points.

✓ In 'Neutral Tones', the narrator feels bitter that their relationship ended. Describing the lover's smile as "the deadest thing" emphasises the narrator's grief now their love has ended. This sense of loss is also evident in the claim "love deceives" — they no longer trust love.

4) However, make sure you <u>only</u> use words that you know the <u>meaning</u> of. For example, don't say that a poem uses '<u>anaphora</u>' if you don't know what it <u>really means</u> — it will be <u>obvious</u> to the examiner.

Use technical terms where possible

1) To get top marks, you need to use the <u>correct technical terms</u> when you're writing about poetry.

2) There's a handy <u>glossary</u> at the back of this book that <u>explains</u> these terms.

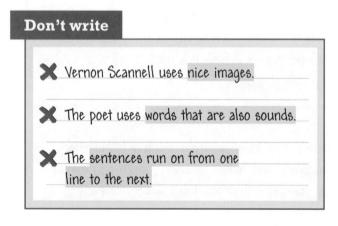

Don't write

✗ Vernon Scannell uses nice images.

✗ The poet uses words that are also sounds.

✗ The sentences run on from one line to the next.

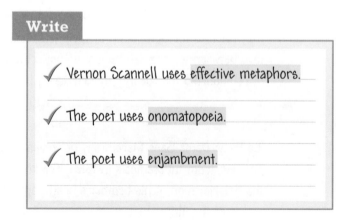

Write

✓ Vernon Scannell uses effective metaphors.

✓ The poet uses onomatopoeia.

✓ The poet uses enjambment.

Planning Your Answer

In an exam, it's always tempting to launch straight into writing your answer, but this can end in disaster. Making a plan is the key to a sophisticated, well-structured essay. Trust me — it's worth it.

In the exam, spend five minutes planning your answer

1) Plan your answer before you start writing — that way, you're less likely to forget something important.

2) Write your plan at the top of your answer booklet and draw a neat line through it when you've finished.

3) Don't spend too long on your plan. It's only rough work, so you don't need to write in full sentences. Here are a few examples of different ways you can plan your answer:

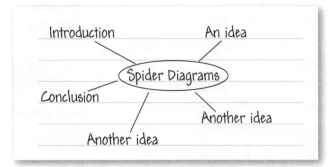

Bullet points with...
- Intro...
- An idea...
- The next idea...

Tables with...

A point...	Quote to back this up...
Another point...	Quote...
A different point...	Quote...

4) A good plan will help you organise your ideas — and write a good, well-structured essay.

Here's a sample question and plan

Q8 Compare how poets present family relationships in 'A Child to his Sick Grandfather' and in **one** other poem from 'Relationships'. **[20 marks]**

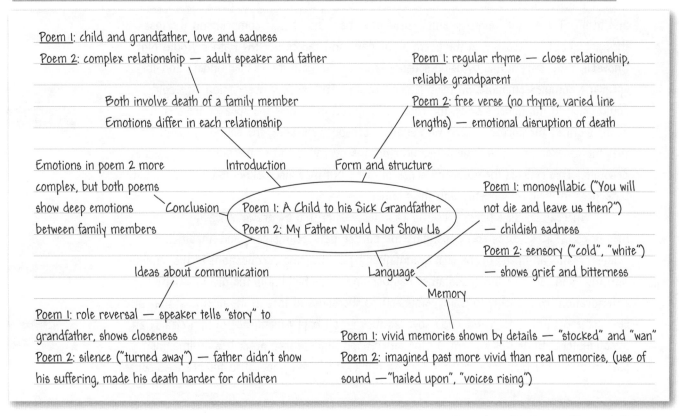

Sample Answer

Here's how you could use the plan on page 67 to write a really good answer.

'A Child to his Sick Grandfather' and 'My Father Would Not Show Us' both explore the relationship between two family members of different generations, and how these relationships are affected by death. However, the relationships presented differ due to the individuals involved and the different emotions in each relationship. 'A Child to his Sick Grandfather' is written from the perspective of a young child: the poem shows the child's love for their grandfather and their sorrow when he dies. In contrast, 'My Father Would Not Show Us' focuses on an adult speaker's complex relationship with their father and their final interaction with his body after he has died. Despite their differences, both poems show the strong feelings and emotions involved in family relationships.

Both poets use form and structure to emphasise elements of love between the two family members in each relationship. Baillie uses a regular AABBCC rhyme scheme — the couplets parallel the close bond of the two family members in the poem, and the consistent rhyme scheme reflects the reliable, comforting presence the grandfather has been in the child's life. This shows how strong the connection between the two family members is, and makes the grandfather's approaching death more moving to the reader. Unlike Baillie's poem, de Kok's poem is written in free verse. The lack of rhyme scheme and varied line lengths imply that the father's death leaves the speaker struggling to control their thoughts and feelings. This emotional disturbance suggests that the speaker had underlying, if complex, feelings of love for their father. Both poets therefore use form to suggest aspects of closeness in the familial relationships they portray.

Both poems also use language to convey the particular feelings that can surround the end of a familial relationship. In 'A Child to his Sick Grandfather', the speaker uses simple, monosyllabic language, e.g. "You will not die and leave us then?". This accentuates their childish innocence and feelings of concern as they see their grandfather grow "old and frail". The simple language emphasises how they cannot fully comprehend the loss they are about to face, giving the poem a poignant and sad tone. 'My Father Would Not Show Us' differs from this by using sensory language to help the reader understand the speaker's complex emotions on their father's death. The sensory description "It's cold" could refer to the father's body, the room it is stored in or how the speaker feels chilled at the sight of the corpse. Along with another sensory reference, the sound of "white" that the speaker imagines their father hearing, the overall mood of the poem is bleak and desolate. This reflects the speaker's sense of grief, but may also acknowledge the implicit bitterness in their relationship with their father.

Whereas Baillie's poem presents a family relationship by drawing heavily on memories, de Kok's does so by spanning the border between memory and imagination. Baillie creates an image of the sick grandfather by contrasting recollections of his "smile" with the "wan" spectre the grandfather has become. This highlights the grandfather's deterioration from vitality to frailty, emphasising the sense of loss in the poem. It may also reveal the depth of the grandchild's love, as they recall happy memories of him clearly and affectionately. In de Kok's poem, on the other hand, the speaker describes an imagined past more vividly than their real memories. For example, they appeal to the reader's sense

Marginal notes:

Refer to the question and the poems you're writing about in your opening sentence.

Sum up how the poems relate to the theme.

Compare the poem's form

Explain how each point relates to the question.

Remember to develop each point.

Comment on similarities and differences between the poems.

Use the correct technical terms.

Integrate examples into your sentences.

Keep making comparisons between the poems.

Give a personal response.

Sample Answer

of hearing by envisioning "a house with a tin roof / being hailed upon" and "voices rising" within the house. This sensory language gives the reader a clear sense of a happy, lively childhood, but the fact that it is imagined and only what "might have been" emphasises how silent and unhappy the speaker's childhood may have actually been. This suggests that the speaker may feel deprived of childhood experiences, and adds to the underlying feelings of frustration in their complicated relationship with their father.

> Comment on the language the poets use, and the effect it has.

Both poems explore ideas about communication in family relationships, but from different perspectives. Baillie's poem inverts usual familial roles by showing the speaker's progression from being looked after by their grandfather at the start of the poem to offering to tell "a story" to the grandfather at the end. This shows the child adopting a role that it's likely the grandfather once occupied. Stories about animals and knights were commonly told to children in the 18th century, which may suggest the child is retelling stories told to them in the past and familiar to the grandfather. This shows how they are trying to comfort him and remind him of happy memories, emphasising how close and loving their bond is. On the other hand, de Kok's speaker refers to a lack of communication as their father approached death — "he turned away" from his children as he began to die. This suggests a lack of closeness, although it may also be that the father did not want to distress his children by letting them see him suffer. This breakdown in communication between the father and his children further highlights the complexity of their relationship, as while the father's behaviour could have been motivated by love, it also made his death more painful for his children. In each poem, the type and extent of family communication reflects the nature of the relationships that they show.

> Make sure you mention structure.

> Bring in wider knowledge where you can.

> Suggest more than one interpretation of the poem.

> Explain how each point relates to the question.

Both poems portray the different emotions involved in family relationships through the context of the death of a family member. Baillie's loving relationship ends in sadness, whereas de Kok's more complex relationship combines elements of love with negative feelings of frustration. Despite these differences, both poems show the powerful emotions family relationships evoke and how the trauma of death can enhance their intensity.

> Your last sentence should sum up your argument, and it needs to be memorable.

How to write a top grade answer

There's no single way of getting a grade 9, but these handy hints will help you on your way:

1) Be original — examiners get bored of reading the same thing over and over again, so coming up with your own interpretations will impress them (as long as you can back up your ideas with evidence).

2) Be critical — this means giving your own opinions about the poems. For example:

> The phrase "God-curst sun" compels the reader to experience the scene as Hardy's narrator does: a bleak, lifeless landscape, devoid of hope and forsaken by God.

3) Get to grips with context. It's not enough just to mention a link to context — you need to really explore the effect it has on the poem, or on your understanding of it. For example:

> Scannell's personal experiences in World War Two add poignancy to the burning of the nettles on the "funeral pyre", and suggest that the speaker respects the power and force of nature, despite their anger.

Section Four — Exam Advice

Adding Quotes and Developing Points

The next couple of pages will give you a chance to practise your P.E.E.D. skills by adding quotes and developing the points in some sample answers. Enjoy...

You can find the answers for this section on p.80.

Complete this plan by adding quotes and developing points

1) Below is an exam question and a plan for answering it.

2) Find quotes from the poems to back up each of the points in the table (marked **A**, **B**, **C** and **D**).

3) Make brief notes on your personal response to each poem (marked **E** and **F**) to complete the plan.

> **Q1**   Compare how poets present romantic love in 'Sonnet 43' and in **one** other poem from 'Relationships'.
>
> [20 marks]

	Sonnet 43	Valentine
Themes and Ideas	Limitless and eternal love.	Realistic portrayal of a loving relationship, honesty.
Language	Religious language ... **(A)** Hyperbole ... **(B)**	Sense of danger ... **(C)** Metaphor ... **(D)**
Form and Structure	Petrarchan sonnet — specific rhyme scheme, iambic pentameter.	Free verse, irregular line lengths, direct address.
Personal Response	**(E)**	**(F)**

Add quotes to improve these answers

In the sample answers below, replace each letter (**A**, **B** and **C**) with a suitable quote.

> **Q2**   Compare how poets present feelings of longing in 'i wanna be yours' and in **one** other poem from 'Relationships'.
>
> [20 marks]

Answer Extract 1

The speakers in 'i wanna be yours' and 'First Date – She / First Date – He' each show a longing for someone. Cooper Clarke emphasises his speaker's need by using imperatives, such as **(A)**. This gives the poem a pleading tone and encourages the reader to recognise the speaker's strong need to be useful. In contrast, Cope uses enjambment to imply that the speakers' desires are distracting, such as when each speaker uses an enjambed sentence to comment on how the other is **(B)**. The sentences flow over three lines, which suggests both speakers have a lack of focus because of their interest in the other person. The male speaker asking **(C)** further emphasises his distraction by showing how little attention he is paying.

Answer Extract 2

In the last stanza of 'i wanna be yours', the speaker repeats the word **(A)**, emphasising their intense longing. This repetition becomes exaggerated in line 27, implying that their feelings are overwhelming. Similarly, Cope repeats phrases in 'First Date – She / First Date – He', such as when each speaker shows concern about having something **(B)**. This suggests that the pair desire each other, as both want to look intelligent to impress the other, even though neither are interested in the music. For example, the woman says she **(C)** about it. Cope highlights how modern romance often involves falsehood and pretence.

Adding Quotes and Developing Points

Have a go at developing these answers

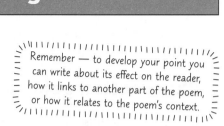

Remember — to develop your point you can write about its effect on the reader, how it links to another part of the poem, or how it relates to the poem's context.

1) Here are some more sample answers to question 2 on p.70.

2) In these extracts, the sentences followed by a letter (**A** or **B**) need to be developed further. Write an extra sentence to develop each point.

> **Q2** Compare how poets present feelings of longing in 'i wanna be yours' and in **one** other poem from 'Relationships'. **[20 marks]**

Answer Extract 1

The first two stanzas of 'i wanna be yours' use an ABABCCCD rhyme scheme to emphasise the strength of the speaker's feelings of longing. The triplet before the final line in these stanzas builds up to the declaration "i wanna be yours", encouraging the reader to keep the speaker's desire in mind as they read the poem. **(A)**. 'First Date – She / First Date – He' also uses rhyme to convey the speakers' feelings. The poems use a regular rhyme scheme (ABCB), which reflects the relationship between the two speakers. The rhyming lines suggest a connection between the two speakers, highlighting their mutual desire, but the unrhymed lines emphasise that they are not completely in sync as a couple. **(B)**.

Answer Extract 2

Both 'i wanna be yours' and 'First Date – She / First Date – He' use references to the ordinary and everyday to reveal the speakers' feelings. Cooper Clarke uses everyday objects like a "teddy bear" and an "electric meter" to create simple, heartfelt metaphors that show the reader how the speaker is desperate to offer even the most banal aspects of their life to their love. **(A)**. On the other hand, Cope's male speaker mentions that "The traffic was dreadful this evening". Although he is "besotted" with the woman, this reference to something as ordinary as being delayed by traffic suggests that his feelings of longing are disrupted by everyday emotions such as nervousness. **(B)**.

Answer Extract 3

Both poets use voice to help convey a sense of longing. 'i wanna be yours' is an extended plea from the speaker to their love. It is written in the first person, but by not capitalising the first-person pronoun "i", the speaker emphasises how their longing for the addressee is so intense that they consider their own importance to be secondary. **(A)**. On the other hand, the first-person viewpoints of 'First Date – She / First Date – He' show the speakers' internal thoughts and concerns, such as the man's concerns about the woman being out of his "league". By using a form that reveals the speakers' internalised worries the poet shows how desperate they are for the date to succeed. **(B)**.

Mark Scheme

Over the next few pages, you're going to put your examiner's hat on (I know, it's a dream come true) and mark some sample answers. This will help you to see what you need to do to get a great mark in your exam.

This section gets you to mark a range of sample answers

1) <u>Marking</u> sample exam answers is a <u>great way</u> to find out <u>exactly</u> what you need to do in the exam to get the grade you want.

2) Most of the answers in this section are only <u>extracts</u>, not <u>full answers</u>. The essay you'll write in the exam will be <u>longer</u> — more like the one on pages 75-76.

3) The mark scheme below is <u>similar</u> to the one that the <u>examiners will use</u> to mark your exam answers.

4) Read the mark scheme <u>thoroughly</u> and make sure that you <u>understand everything</u>.

5) Once you <u>understand</u> the mark scheme, use it to mark the sample exam answers on the next few pages. Don't forget to <u>explain</u> why you chose each grade.

Use this mark scheme to mark the sample answers

Grade band	What is written
8-9	• Shows an insightful and original comparison of the two poems • Effectively integrates a full range of precise examples to support interpretations • Closely analyses the poets' use of language, structure and form, making effective use of technical terms throughout • Gives a detailed exploration of how the poets' techniques affect the reader • Convincingly explores original and alternative interpretations of the ideas, themes, attitudes and context of the poems
6-7	• Presents a carefully thought out, developed comparison of the two poems • Integrates well-chosen examples to support interpretations • Explores the poets' use of language, structure and form, using correct technical terms • Examines the way the techniques used in the poems affect the reader • Gives careful consideration to the ideas, themes, attitudes and context of the poems, offering some original interpretations
4-5	• Gives a clear comparison of the two poems • Provides relevant detail to support interpretations of the poems • Explains how the poets have used some features of language, structure and form, using some relevant technical terms • Comments on how some of the techniques used in the poems affect the reader • Shows a clear understanding of the ideas, themes, attitudes and context of the poems

You can also be awarded <u>grades 1-3</u>. We <u>haven't included</u> any <u>sample answer extracts</u> at 1-3 level though — so those grades aren't in this mark scheme.

Marking Answer Extracts

Here's your first set of sample answers. For each one, think about where it fits in the mark scheme on page 72. Most answers won't fit the criteria for any one band exactly — it's about finding the best fit.

Have a go at marking these answer extracts

For each extract:

a)   Write down the grade band (4-5, 6-7 or 8-9) you think the answer falls into.

b)   Give at least two reasons why you chose that grade band.

> **Q3**   Compare how a child's views about their parents are presented
> in 'One Flesh' and in **one** other poem from 'Relationships'.   **[20 marks]**

Answer Extract 1

Both 'One Flesh' and 'My Father Would Not Show Us' use form and structure to reflect meaning. In de Kok's poem, form reflects the speaker's emotional state after their father's death, whereas in 'One Flesh' it symbolises the parents' relationship over time. The first two stanzas in 'One Flesh' end with a couplet, but not the final stanza — instead it continues the alternate rhyme scheme. This reflects how the speaker feels their parents have grown apart over time. In contrast, 'My Father Would Not Show Us' is written in free verse, with irregular stanza lengths. This emphasises the speaker's changing thoughts — they go from simple restrained observations, like "It's cold in here", to more emotive ideas, imagining how their childhood "might have been". This suggests that the speaker is unsure how to feel about their father after his death.

Answer Extract 2

Both poets show a child who doesn't fully understand their parent or parents. Jennings's speaker doesn't reach a conclusion about their parents' relationship. She writes about how they are both "Strangely apart" and "strangely close", and the final stanza ends with a question. This shows the reader that the speaker is confused by their parents' behaviour. In 'My Father Would Not Show Us', de Kok's speaker explains that the father "hid, he hid away." This uses repetition to show how they can't stop thinking about their father's behaviour in his final days. This hints that the speaker doesn't understand why their father did what he did, and makes it seem like they can't decide whether or not to feel sorry for him.

Answer Extract 3

Both poets use sensory language to show each speaker's feelings about their parent or parents. In 'One Flesh', the poet invokes the reader's sense of touch with the phrase "How cool they lie." The word "cool" suggests that the speaker thinks of their parents as reserved and indifferent, and the appeal to the sense of touch emphasises the speaker's perception that their separation is physical as well as emotional. The word "lie" also implies a communicative breakdown — the poet could be using wordplay to hint that the parents lie to each other. While Jennings uses sensory language to characterise a couple's relationship, de Kok uses it to hint at the speaker's views of their father in his final days. By referring to a "tunnelling sound", de Kok engages the sense of hearing to present the speaker's perception of the father's mindset as he was dying. The "tunnelling" sounds unpleasantly repetitive, suggesting that the speaker believes their father was suffering; the use of sensory language helps the reader to imagine his discomfort. It could also evoke a repetitive beat, like a gravedigger at work, reflecting how the speaker is digging deeper into their father's memories.

Marking Answer Extracts

You must be getting the hang of this now — if you get much more practice you'll be putting those English examiners out of a job. Remember to look out for comparison of the two poems in these extracts.

Have a go at marking these answer extracts

For each extract:

Remember to keep looking back at the mark scheme on page 72.

a) Write down the grade band (4-5, 6-7 or 8-9) you think the answer falls into.

b) Give at least two reasons why you chose that grade band.

> **Q4** Compare how poets use nature to present relationships in 'Nettles' and in **one** other poem from 'Relationships'.　　**[20 marks]**

Answer Extract 1

　　　　Both 'Nettles' and 'She Walks in Beauty' use nature to emphasise one person's powerful love for another. In 'Nettles', Scannell transforms the "nettle bed" into a "regiment" of soldiers who attack the speaker's son. This personification of nature makes the nettles seem threatening. When the speaker later chops down the nettles, it emphasises their love for their son — they confronted an 'army' to protect him. In contrast, Byron likens his female subject to the natural world, comparing her to a "night / Of cloudless climes". The reference to the sky could suggest that she is awe-inspiring, while "cloudless" hints at her perfection. This comparison to flawless nature shows the speaker's admiration for the woman he describes. It also links the woman to the heavens, further emphasising the speaker's strong admiration to the reader.

Answer Extract 2

　　　　Both poets use form to emphasise the link between nature and relationships. 'Nettles' has a single stanza written in iambic pentameter with a regular ABAB rhyme scheme. This steady rhythm imitates the unstoppable beat of a military "parade", which emphasises the threat that nature (the nettles) poses to the boy, and helping the reader to understand why the father is so protective of their child. The rhythm could also be seen to mimic a steady heartbeat, emphasising the father's natural and unwavering love. Meanwhile, Byron's use of a regular alternate rhyme scheme reflects the perfect harmony of darkness and light in nature, and emphasises the mixture of light and dark natural imagery that is used to describe the woman: although there is darkness in her "like the night", she is compared to "starry" skies, which provide light. By using a form that provides a similar balance, Byron emphasises the importance of such harmony to the reader — the woman's embodiment of both light and dark aspects of nature is key to her beauty.

Answer Extract 3

　　　　Both poems use nature to show strong feelings in relationships. In 'Nettles', the parent has "soothed" their son and "slashed in fury" at the nettles, all because they stung the son. Nature is used to show the power of love — it emphasises that loving relationships can involve extremes of tenderness and anger. On the other hand, in 'She Walks in Beauty', Byron uses natural imagery to emphasise the woman's perfection. The animal imagery used when describing each lock of her hair as a "raven tress" links her to nature and helps the reader to imagine her as a naturally beautiful woman.

Marking a Whole Answer

New page, new question and answer. Only this time it's the whole answer, not just an extract...

Now try marking this whole answer

Make sure you've read the mark scheme on page 72.

a) Write down the grade band (4-5, 6-7 or 8-9) you think the answer falls into.

b) Give at least four reasons why you chose that grade band.

> **Q5** Compare how poets present the loss of love in 'Neutral Tones' and in **one** other poem from 'Relationships'. **[20 marks]**

'Neutral Tones' and 'A Complaint' both focus on the end of a relationship and the feelings that this loss of love produces. Both poets use imagery to convey how the speakers feel when love is lost, and Hardy even uses imagery of death to present a sense of grief. Both poets also convey how the memory of a lost love can endure over time, and both directly address the objects of their love. Although Wordsworth's speaker is perhaps more focused on their own emotions than Hardy's, both poems ultimately show the traumatic impact that the loss of love has had on the speakers in the poem.

Both poets use form and structure to emphasise the sorrow and pain of lost love. In 'Neutral Tones', the poem begins and ends with "a pond edged with grayish leaves". This cyclical structure demonstrates that the speaker is unable to overcome their feelings of pessimism and hopelessness at the breakdown of their relationship. This is reinforced by the regular ABBA rhyme scheme — the repetition of the A rhyme at the start and end of each stanza hints that they cannot break free from the memory of their loss. The structure of 'A Complaint' also reflects the unchanging nature of the speaker's sorrow. The repetition of "poor" in the first and last lines creates a sense of circularity, which shows how long-lasting the speaker's torment is and suggests that they too replay thoughts in their mind. Both poets also use a largely regular rhythm: in Hardy's poem, this slows the pace and encourages the reader to identify with the speaker's feelings of depression, whereas in Wordsworth's poem it propels the poem relentlessly onwards, hinting at the speaker's single-minded obsession with their loss.

Hardy and Wordsworth both use vivid imagery to convey the sorrow experienced at the loss of love. Hardy uses imagery of death — the entire landscape is colourless, suggesting that nothing is living. The leaves are "gray" and even the sun, normally a symbol of warmth and life, is "white" and cold. This reflects both the death of the speaker's relationship and the desolation they feel at the loss. Moreover, the "deadest thing" is the "smile" of their lover; this superlative hints that, while the rest of the world merely appears dead, their relationship stands no chance of resurrection. In Wordsworth's poem, on the other hand, water imagery is used to describe the speaker's love. However, it changes over the course of the poem, which reflects the change in the speaker's relationship. By initially describing feelings of love as a dynamic and lively "fountain", they reveal how exciting their love was, before revealing that now the "waters sleep" in a "hidden well". Water in a well can be hard to access — this shows the reader how their love has become strained. This contrast emphasises the sense of loss that the speaker now feels.

Both speakers address someone directly, which makes the poems seem more personal. In the first

This answer continues on page 76.

Section Five — Improving and Marking Sample Answers

Marking a Whole Answer

stanza of 'Neutral Tones', Hardy's speaker refers only to the collective "We"; in the second stanza they refer to themselves and their lover both as a couple ("us") and as individuals ("Your eyes on me"); and in the third and fourth stanzas they are referred to solely as individuals. This may reflect the gradual breakdown of their relationship, or the speaker's dawning realisation on "that winter day" that they had lost their lover. In contrast, Wordsworth's speaker refers directly to his addressee only once, at the start of the poem ("Your love"). In combination with the frequent usage of the first-person pronoun "I", this hints at the speaker's self-absorption and suggests that their emotions are so overwhelming that they can only focus on themselves. The subject-verb inversion in stanza two ("Blest was I") further highlights this by putting emphasis on the "I" and therefore on the speaker's personal feelings. This personal, direct tone reflects the possible context of both poems, as both may have been about real events. 'Neutral Tones' may well be autobiographical in nature, as Hardy was known to have an unhappy first marriage, whilst some critics believe that Wordsworth wrote 'A Complaint' about his friend Samuel Taylor Coleridge after Coleridge became addicted to drugs and withdrew from the pair's joint projects and friendship.

Both poems use sound to emphasise the painful sorrow of loss, and the longevity of this feeling. Hardy uses alliteration in the phrase "wrings with wrong" to create a vivid sense of how the loss torments the speaker. In addition, the assonance of the long 'oh' sound in words such as "rove", "Over" and "ago" in the second stanza lengthens the sound of the words, emphasising how "tedious" their former lover now finds them, and hinting that the loss of the speaker's lover has damaged their confidence and self-belief. Similarly, Wordsworth's speaker repeats the rhymes "poor" and "door", with the assonance of the long vowel sounds hinting at how long and dreary life seems without love. Wordsworth also repeats an 'ing' sound when describing the fountain as "murmuring, sparkling, living", which creates a sense of dynamism — but this trace of life only emphasises the speaker's anguish that the same love now lies "In silence".

The speakers of both poems hold others responsible for the pain they are enduring, perhaps hinting at the condemnation and bitterness that can stem from lost love. Hardy's speaker seems to blame their lover for the end of their relationship — their description of their lover's "grin of bitterness" hints at their belief that their lover took pleasure in causing them pain. By referring to the "God-curst sun", they could even be suggesting that God is to blame for their suffering, or indicating that the loss they experienced has blighted their life to the extent that even the sun seems "curst". Similarly, Wordsworth's speaker states how the love they experienced flowed without "taking heed" of the speaker's "need". This comparison to a powerful flow of water suggests that the speaker didn't believe they could control the love. This implies that the speaker thinks they aren't responsible for the love's failure and encourages the reader to see them as a victim.

'Neutral Tones' and 'A Complaint' present vivid depictions of the long-lasting emotional turmoil caused by the loss of love. Both compare the end of a relationship to a form of death or stillness, highlighting the grief that such a loss can cause, and both are intrinsically pessimistic in outlook, which is reflected in each poem's structure and form. As such, both poems convey a highly personal account of their speakers' lost loves, in a way that parallels the poets' own experiences of loss and unhappiness.

Glossary

alliteration	Where words that are close together start with the same sound, e.g. "wrings with wrong".
ambiguity	Where a word or phrase has two or more possible interpretations.
anaphora	Where a word or phrase is repeated at the start of consecutive sentences or lines.
antithesis	Where the contrast between two ideas is emphasised by using a repeated structure, e.g. "One shade the more, one ray the less".
assonance	When words share the same vowel sound but their consonants are different, e.g. "Which waves in every raven tress".
autobiographical	Describing something that happened in the poet's life.
ballad	A form of poetry that tells a story and can often be set to music.
caesura (plural caesurae)	A pause in a line of poetry. E.g. after the full stop in "How cool they lie. They hardly ever touch".
chronological	When events are arranged in the order in which they happened.
contraction	A new word made by joining two words together, usually with an apostrophe, e.g. "Will't".
cyclical structure	Where key elements at the start of the text repeat themselves at the end.
dialect	A variation of a language spoken by people from a particular place or background. Dialects might include different words or sentence constructions, e.g. "I wot not how it be".
direct address	When the narrator speaks directly to the reader or another character, e.g. "its zookeeper – you".
dramatic monologue	A form of poetry that uses the assumed voice of a single speaker who is not the poet to address an implied audience, e.g. 'My Last Duchess'.
ellipsis	A set of three dots which indicate a pause. It can add to a poem's meaning, e.g. in 'Neutral Tones', an ellipsis indicates that time has passed.
emotive	Something that makes you feel a particular emotion.
end-stopping	Finishing a line of poetry with the end of a phrase or sentence.
enjambment	When a sentence or phrase runs over from one line or stanza to the next.
figurative language	Language that is used in a non-literal way to create an effect, e.g. personification.
first person	When a poet writes about themselves or their group, using words like "I", "my", "we" and "our".
form	The type of poem, e.g. a sonnet or a ballad, and its features, like number of lines, rhyme and rhythm.
free verse	Poetry that doesn't rhyme and has no regular rhythm or line length.
half-rhymes	Words that have a similar, but not identical, end sound. E.g. "hurt" and "heart".
hyperbole	The use of exaggeration to emphasise a point.
iambic pentameter	Poetry with a metre of ten syllables — five of them stressed, and five unstressed. The stress falls on every second syllable, e.g. "My soul can reach, when feeling out of sight".
iambic tetrameter	Like iambic pentameter but with a metre of eight syllables — four stressed and four unstressed. E.g. "There is a change — and I am poor;".
imagery	Language that creates a picture in your mind. It includes metaphors, similes and personification.
interjection	A word or phrase that interrupts the flow of a sentence, e.g. "I know not how" in 'My Last Duchess'.
internal rhyme	When two or more words rhyme, and at least one word isn't at the end of a line. The rhyming words can be in the same line or nearby lines. E.g. "And then I took my billhook".
irony	When words are used to imply the opposite of what they normally mean. It can also mean when there is a difference between what people expect and what actually happens.

Glossary

juxtaposition	When a poet puts two ideas, events, characters or descriptions <u>close to each other</u> to encourage the reader to <u>contrast</u> them. E.g. "<u>diagnosis</u>" and "<u>prognosis</u>" in 'Love's Dog'.
language	The <u>choice of words</u> used. Different kinds of language have <u>different effects</u>.
metaphor	A way of describing something by saying that it <u>is something else</u>, e.g. "time itself's a feather". An <u>extended metaphor</u> is a metaphor that is <u>carried on</u>, e.g. the onion in 'Valentine'.
metre	The arrangement of stressed and unstressed syllables to create <u>rhythm</u> in a line of poetry.
monologue	<u>One person</u> speaking alone for a long period of time.
monosyllable	Words with only <u>one syllable</u>, e.g. "I love my own old dad."
mood	The <u>feel</u> or <u>atmosphere</u> of a poem, e.g. humorous, peaceful, fearful.
narrative	Writing that tells a <u>story</u>, e.g. 'Nettles'.
narrator	The <u>person</u> speaking the words. E.g. the narrator of 'My Last Duchess' is the Duke.
onomatopoeia	A word that <u>sounds like</u> the thing it's describing, e.g. "slashed" in 'Nettles'.
oxymoron	A phrase which appears to <u>contradict</u> itself, e.g. "<u>Alive</u> enough to have strength to <u>die</u>".
personification	Describing a non-living thing as if it has <u>human qualities</u> and <u>feelings</u>, or <u>behaves</u> in a human way, e.g. "the starving sod".
Petrarchan sonnet	A form of <u>sonnet</u> in which the first eight lines have a regular ABBA rhyme scheme and <u>introduce</u> a problem, while the final six lines have a different rhyme scheme and <u>solve</u> the problem.
plosive	A <u>short burst of sound</u> made when you say a word containing the letters b, d, g, k, p or t.
refrain	A line or phrase which is <u>repeated</u> throughout a poem, often at the <u>end</u> of a stanza. E.g. "i wanna be yours".
rhetorical question	A <u>question</u> that doesn't need an answer, but is asked to <u>make</u> or <u>emphasise</u> a point.
rhyme scheme	A <u>pattern</u> of rhyming words in a poem. E.g. 'First Date – She / First Date – He' has an <u>ABCB</u> rhyme scheme — this means that the <u>second</u> and <u>fourth</u> lines in each stanza rhyme.
rhyming couplet	A <u>pair of rhyming lines</u> that are next to each other, e.g. lines 1 and 2 of 'The Manhunt'.
rhythm	A <u>pattern of sounds</u> created by the arrangement of <u>stressed</u> and <u>unstressed</u> syllables.
sibilance	Repetition of '<u>s</u>' and / or '<u>sh</u>' sounds, e.g. "thoughts <u>s</u>erenely <u>s</u>weet expre<u>ss</u>".
simile	A way of describing something by <u>comparing</u> it to something else, usually by using the words "like" or "as", e.g. "Silence between them <u>like a thread</u> to hold".
sonnet	A form of poem with <u>fourteen lines</u> that usually follows a <u>clear rhyme scheme</u>.
stanza	A <u>group of lines</u> in a poem.
structure	The <u>order</u> and <u>arrangement</u> of ideas and events in a poem, e.g. how it begins, develops and ends.
syllable	A single <u>unit of sound</u> within a word. E.g. "all" has one syllable, "always" has two.
symbolism	When an object <u>stands for something else</u>. E.g. the fountain in 'A Complaint' symbolises love.
synesthesia	The <u>linking</u> of two or more <u>senses</u> for effect, e.g. "everything he hears is white".
third person	When a poet writes about a character who <u>isn't</u> the narrator, using words like "<u>he</u>" or "<u>she</u>".
tone	The <u>mood</u> or <u>feelings</u> suggested by the way the narrator <u>writes</u>, e.g. bitter, reflective.
voice	The <u>characteristics</u> of the <u>person</u> narrating the poem. Poems are usually written either using the poet's voice, as if they're speaking to you <u>directly</u>, or the voice of a <u>character</u>.

Index

A

adoration 7, 9, 13, 23, 41
alliteration 6, 8, 10, 18, 26, 30, 45, 54, 64, 76
ambiguity 5, 23, 25, 30, 58, 65
anaphora 12, 13, 25, 41, 50, 63
anger 14, 15, 26, 27, 36, 39, 43, 51, 54, 69, 74

B

ballad 3, 49, 55
beauty 2, 3, 6, 7, 16, 36, 49, 52, 54, 74
bitterness 8, 10, 11, 25, 39, 45, 54, 56, 66-68, 76
bleak settings 2, 3, 10, 11, 39, 42, 44, 45, 53, 57, 69

C

caesurae 2, 12, 16, 20, 37, 44, 51
'Child to his Sick Grandfather, A' 4, 5, 21, 27, 31, 38-40, 42, 53, 56, 58, 64, 67-69
colour 10, 11, 30, 45, 53, 75
'Complaint, A' 8, 9, 29, 31, 36, 39, 41, 44, 49, 51, 53-55, 57, 58, 65, 75, 76
context 62, 63, 65, 69, 71, 72
contrasts 2, 3, 5-9, 18, 20, 22, 24, 26, 27, 36, 38, 49, 52, 53, 57, 75
couplets 4, 9, 15, 21, 24, 25, 28, 29, 36, 37, 49, 50, 55, 58, 68, 73
cyclical structure 3, 11, 44, 55, 58, 75

D

danger 2, 3, 15, 18, 19, 36, 42, 45, 51, 52, 65, 70
death 2, 4, 5, 11-15, 18, 19, 30, 31, 38, 42, 43, 49, 51, 53, 56, 58, 64, 65, 67-69, 73, 75, 76
desire 3, 7, 13, 15, 17, 22, 23, 36, 40, 50, 56, 65, 70, 71
destructive love 3, 36, 40, 42, 51, 53
direct address 4, 5, 8, 9, 11, 12, 19, 22, 24, 56, 70, 75, 76
distance 9, 17, 20, 21, 29, 31, 44, 50, 51, 57, 62, 73

E

end-stopping 18, 50, 51
enjambment 7, 8, 10, 12, 14, 15, 18, 27-29, 36, 50, 66, 70

F

family relationships 5, 27, 31, 37, 38, 67-69, 73
fear 20, 24, 30, 45
'First Date – She / First Date – He' 16, 17, 21, 40, 44, 45, 49-51, 56, 58, 70, 71

first-person narrators 13, 19, 24, 31, 56, 71, 76
forms of poetry 49
free verse 31, 49, 67, 68, 70, 73

G

growing older 4, 5, 21, 38, 53

H

honesty 19, 23, 24, 37, 42, 54, 70
hopelessness 2, 3, 11, 44, 45, 75
humour 17, 23, 52
hyperbole 13, 41, 50, 70

I

'i wanna be yours' 7, 13, 15, 22, 23, 37, 38, 40, 41, 50, 52, 56, 70, 71
iambic pentameter 13, 15, 27, 49, 55, 70, 74
iambic tetrameter 3, 7, 9, 55
imagery 2, 3, 6, 7, 9, 10, 20-29, 31, 37, 41-44, 52, 53, 74, 75
irony 15-17, 26, 50, 51

L

'La Belle Dame Sans Merci' 2, 3, 17, 40, 41, 43-45, 49, 55, 57, 58, 65
longing 3, 7, 13, 15, 17, 23, 40, 70, 71
loss 2, 3, 8, 9, 31, 36, 42, 43, 53, 55, 66-68, 75, 76
'Love's Dog' 11, 23-25, 37, 43, 45, 50, 53-55, 63, 66

M

'Manhunt, The' 9, 27-29, 37-39, 43, 50, 52, 58, 64
memory 3, 5, 9-11, 27, 29, 31, 39, 51, 54, 55, 67-69, 73, 75
metaphors 2, 8, 9, 18-22, 28, 29, 38, 52, 53, 64, 66, 70, 71
monologues 15, 17
monosyllabic words 4, 5, 23, 54, 55, 57, 67, 68
'My Father Would Not Show Us' 5, 25, 30, 31, 37-39, 42, 49, 51, 54, 56, 58, 67-69, 73
'My Last Duchess' 14, 15, 19, 36, 40, 43, 50, 51, 55-58, 64

N

nature 6-8, 11, 26, 27, 45, 69, 74
negative emotions 11, 12, 21, 24, 25, 45, 54, 69
'Nettles' 5, 26, 27, 29, 37-39, 43, 51, 52, 54, 55, 57, 69, 74

'Neutral Tones' 3, 10, 11, 25, 39, 42, 44, 45, 53, 55-57, 66, 69, 75, 76
nontraditional love 3, 13, 18, 19, 22, 23, 25, 37, 49, 52, 54, 57

O

obsession 3, 15, 65, 75
'One Flesh' 11, 17, 20, 21, 29, 38, 43-45, 51, 53, 57, 62, 73
onomatopoeia 66

P

P.E.E.D. 63
personification 4, 10, 26, 36, 52, 53, 74
Petrarchan sonnet 13, 49, 70
plosive sounds 24, 45, 54, 64
power 2, 14, 15, 18, 22, 26, 27, 36, 40, 43, 50, 56, 69, 74
protectiveness 5, 22, 27, 30, 37, 38, 53, 55, 74
purity 6-8, 12, 36, 41, 49

R

religious language 8, 9, 12, 13, 20, 21, 41, 69, 70, 76
repetition 2-5, 8-10, 12-14, 16-20, 22-25, 28, 30, 31, 40, 41, 43, 44, 50, 53, 56, 58, 70, 73, 75, 76
rhetorical questions 8, 9, 16, 51, 57
Romanticism 2, 3, 8, 9

S

Samuel Taylor Coleridge 9, 65, 76
senses 30, 31, 51, 67-69, 73
separation 3, 9, 20, 21, 44, 51, 57, 58, 73
'She Walks in Beauty' 3, 6, 7, 36, 41, 44, 49, 52, 54, 74
sibilance 4, 6, 54
sickness 2, 4, 5, 24, 25, 40, 42, 43, 57, 65
similes 6, 18, 20-22, 44, 52, 53
simple language 4, 22, 23, 57, 68
'Sonnet 43' 7, 9, 12, 13, 19, 23, 37, 40, 41, 49, 50, 54, 56, 57, 63, 70
sound 54, 76
suffering 2, 3, 10, 11, 19, 25, 27-29, 31, 42, 43, 53, 67, 69, 73, 76
symbolism 2, 8, 18, 19, 22, 25, 37, 39, 43, 49, 50, 73

V

'Valentine' 13, 15, 18, 19, 23, 36, 37, 42, 45, 49, 51, 52, 54-57, 65, 70
voice 2, 5, 31, 56, 71

Answers

These are the answers to the exercises in Section Five. They're only suggestions, so don't worry if what you've written doesn't match exactly — there are lots of possible answers.

Page 70 — Adding Quotes and Developing Points

Sample Plan

(A) "my lost Saints"

(B) "to the depth and breadth and height / My soul can reach"

(C) "Lethal."

(D) "It is a moon wrapped in brown paper."

(E) The poem's enjambment gives the reader the impression that the speaker's outpouring of love is hard to control.

(F) Short and single-word lines make the reader wonder if the speaker is trying not to get carried away by their love.

Answer Extract 1

(A) "let"

(B) "totally into this music"

(C) "Where are we?"

Answer Extract 2

(A) "deep"

(B) "to say"

(C) "couldn't care less"

Page 71 — Adding Quotes and Developing Points

Answer Extract 1

(A) The repetition of "i wanna be yours" also links to the poem's title, reinforcing it as the poem's central message.

(B) The lack of synchronisation is also reflected in how the two speakers often mention the same topics but at different stages in each of the poems.

Answer Extract 2

(A) The everyday nature of many of the objects chosen also ensures that the poem is accessible to a wide range of readers.

(B) The mention of an everyday cause for concern (traffic) also makes the speaker more relatable, so the reader sympathises with him.

Answer Extract 3

(A) This is reinforced at the end of the poem, as the final word is "yours", which suggests that the addressee holds all of the power.

(B) These anxieties around romance are likely to be familiar to a modern audience, making the speakers seem relatable and authentic.

Page 73 — Marking Answer Extracts

Answer Extract 1

I think this would get a grade 6-7 because it gives a developed comparison of the poems and examines the effect of form in both poems. To get a higher grade, the points need to be developed in more detail.

Answer Extract 2

I think this answer would get a grade 4-5. It clearly compares the two poems, and supports the point with quotes. To get a higher grade, the comparisons need to be developed in more detail.

Answer Extract 3

I would give this answer a grade 8-9 because it gives a detailed analysis of the poet's use of language, uses the correct technical vocabulary and suggests an original alternative interpretation of an example.

Page 74 — Marking Answer Extracts

Answer Extract 1

I would give this extract a grade 6-7 because it makes a point, gives well-chosen examples from the poems and analyses language clearly. To get a higher grade, the point needs to be developed more, e.g. it could consider how it relates to the poems' context.

Answer Extract 2

I think this answer would get a grade 8-9 because it integrates examples from the poems, explains them effectively with plenty of technical terms, and develops the points thoroughly.

Answer Extract 3

I think this answer would get a grade 4-5. This is because it makes a point comparing the poems and backs it up with examples that are explained. To get a higher grade it needs to offer more explanation of how the quotes support the point.

Pages 75-76 — Marking a Whole Answer

I think this answer should be awarded a grade 8-9 because it makes a wide range of detailed, original comparisons, analyses the effects of form, structure and language on the reader, and gives well-integrated, precise examples of the poets' techniques. It also explores the context of both poems.

AREHR41